About the Author

Jost Andreas Loewe (b. 1973)

The Very Revd Dr Andreas Loewe is Dean of St Paul's Cathedral Melbourne. He is a Fellow of the Royal Historical Society and a Senior Fellow of the Conservatorium of Music, The University of Melbourne. An expert on Protestant German History and the sacred music of Johann Sebastian Bach, he has previously published on Bach, Bonhoeffer, Luther and the Reformation for academic, church and public audiences.

HEART WORK

Working Deeper, Not Harder

ANDREAS LOEWE

St Paul's Press
MELBOURNE

Published by St Paul's Press
An imprint of St Paul's Cathedral Melbourne
209 Flinders Lane
Melbourne VIC 3000
Australia

www.cathedralshopmelbourne.com | www.cathedral.org.au/press

Copyright © Andreas Loewe, 2025. All rights reserved.

ISBN 978-1-7640816-0-3 (hardcover), ISBN 978-1-7640816-1-0 (ebook)

Andreas Loewe asserts his right under section 193 of the *Copyright Act 1968* (Cth) to be identified as the author of this work.

Scripture quotations are taken from the *New Revised Standard Version Bible*, Anglicised Edition, copyright © 1989 the Division of Christian Education of the National Council of the Churches of Christ in the United States of America. Used by permission. All rights reserved.

Quotations from Dietrich Bonhoeffer's poetry are taken from Andreas Loewe and Katherine Firth, *Journeying with Bonhoeffer: Six Steps on the Path of Discipleship* (Melbourne: Acorn Press, 2024), and were translated from the original German by Katherine Firth.

Quotations from Johann Sebastian Bach's *St John Passion* are taken from Andreas Loewe, *Johann Sebastian Bach's St John Passion (BWV 245): A Theological Commentary—With a New Study Translation by Katherine Firth and a Preface by N.T. Wright* (Leiden: Royal Brill, 2014), and were translated from the original German by Katherine Firth.

Apart from any fair dealing for the purposes of private study, research, criticism or review, no part of this publication may be reproduced, stored in a retrieval system, or transmitted in any form or by any means, electronic, mechanical, photocopying, recording or otherwise, without the prior permission of the publisher.

A catalogue record for this book is available from the National Library of Australia.

This edition first published in 2025.

For my family, and the St Paul's Cathedral community, who shared my journey.

In memory of Sister Benedicta Ward SLG (1933-2022). Eternal memory.

Contents

About the Author	ii
Dedication	v
List of Images	viii
Acknowledgements	ix
Foreword	xi
How to Use this Book	xvii
1 The Inward Journey of Lent	1
2 From Law to Faith	13
3 The Courage to Ask	27
4 Transformation through Trust	41
5 The Aroma of Christ	55
6 The Witnessing Heart	71
7 The Open Heart of God	85
Afterword	101
A Brief Guide for Book Groups	105
Notes and Further Reading	107
Index	125
About this Book	140

List of Images

Cover Image Merrillee, *The Milky Way and Country Landscape*, Gresford, New South Wales. Stock photo ID: 1023383340.

Image 1: Rembrandt Harmenszoon van Rijn (1606-69), *The Return of the Prodigal Son*, Etching, 1636, Gift of Philip Hofer.

Image 2: Hans Baldung Grien (1484-1545), *The Conversion of Paul*, Woodcut, 1514, Rosenwald Collection.

Image 3: Lucas van Leyden (1489/1494-1533), *Queen Esther before Ahasuerus*, Engraving, 1518, Rosenwald Collection.

Image 4: Rembrandt Harmenszoon van Rijn (1606-69), *Abraham's Sacrifice*, Etching and Drypoint, 1655, Rosenwald Collection.

Image 5: Andreas Andreani (1558/9-1629) after Andrea Mantegna (c. 1431-1506), *The Triumph of Julius Caesar*, chiaroscuro woodcut, 1599, Rosenwald Collection.

Image 6: Augustin Hirschvogel (1503-1553), *The Entry into Jerusalem*, Etching, 1547, Rosenwald Collection.

Image 7: Annibale Carracci (1560-1609), *Pietà (The Christ of Caprarola)*, Ethching, Engraving and Drypoint.

Images 1-7 are all from the collection of the National Gallery of Art, Washington D.C., and reproduced by permission.

Acknowledgements

I acknowledge the Wurundjeri People of the Kulin Nation on whose sovereign lands, never ceded, this book was written.

I would like to thank the congregation at St Paul's Cathedral, Melbourne, for the opportunity to develop the first versions of what would become this book with them as part of my Lent preaching and teaching in 2025. In particular, I would like to thank the people who drew on some of the ideas I raised in my talks in their own teaching, intercessions and shaping of worship; those who spoke with me about their own experiences of heart work; and all who encouraged me to turn the material into this book.

Thank you also to my friends and colleagues in Melbourne and Toronto who read the book in advance for their valuable feedback and input: particularly Canon Philippa Lohmeyer-Collins (who, a keen cyclist herself, encouraged me on my gradual progress to fitness), Canon Dr Ruth Redpath AO (who, a medical doctor and a priest, told me to do my physiotherapy exercises 'religiously'), The Revd Brian So (who was the first to pray with me the day after my accident, and with whom I shared my frustration at not making 'sufficient' progress) and Canon Dr Tim Watson (who took on many of my tasks on the days I had to attend physiotherapy, and always would text me with a kind 'how are things going?'). Thank you to Dr Christina McLeish and River Gammon for reading the proofs.

Thank you to my partner and academic collaborator, Dr Katherine Firth, for permission to use her translations of the poems of Bonhoeffer and chorales of Johann Sebastian Bach in this work. Katherine not only cared for me during my injuries and cheered me on in my recovery work, but was, as always, an integral part of the thinking and feeling towards making this book happen. She provided a number of the insights that sparked various chapters, as well as the subtitle to the book as a whole. Our recent joint academic research into heart work was submitted only a few months before my accident, and will be published as part of *The Reception of John's Gospel*, 'John in Bach: receiving and telling the gospel of love in and from the heart' (Baylor University Press, 2027-29).

Finally, thank you to the healthcare professionals who helped me on my journey of healing—the doctors and staff at St Vincent's Hospital Fitzroy, my physiotherapists Jess and Tom, my osteopath Andrew, and my remedial personal trainer Amanda. Thank you for guiding the rehabilitation and healing after my fracture—which gave me the idea for this book.

Foreword

The reflections in this book were delivered as sermons I preached at St Paul's Cathedral Melbourne during Lent 2025. The idea of contrasting 'hard work' with 'heart work' came from an unexpected source—a bicycling accident in which I broke my upper arm just before Lent began.

A kind Uber driver got me and my bike to the Emergency Room of our local hospital, and my partner Katherine met me at the doors with snacks and energy drinks, the start of my three-month recovery and rehab. What followed was a period where I often felt frustration at pain and what I perceived as slow progress, much of which coincided with Lent itself; a physical parallel to the spiritual journey I was exploring with our diverse multi-cultural congregations at the Cathedral.

As I navigated this time of healing, I found myself in an unfamiliar position. Normally active and independent, I was suddenly dependent on others—emergency room doctors who examined my arm and bound up my wounds, physiotherapists who designed my rehabilitation program, my partner at home, and, perhaps most unaccustomed and therefore humbling, the ordinary kindnesses of strangers who held doors open when they saw me with my arm in a sling.

For a priest accustomed to providing care rather than receiving it, this role reversal offered me much food for thought. I tried to make sense of what I was experiencing through the Scriptures and spiritual traditions of the Church. The work of rehabilitation—placing my trust in medical practitioners and following their guidance even when exercises were painful or progress seemed slow—shaped my understanding of what I came to call 'heart work'.

This is the inner transformation that happens when we finally acknowledge that we are not 'fine', that we cannot heal ourselves, and that we need help. God's help, primarily, but also the help that comes through the human hands and hearts that God places in our lives.

Each chapter in this book explores a different dimension of this heart work. We begin by examining the fundamental contrast between outward achievement and inward renewal. From there, we explore how Christ makes God's word accessible to our hearts, how we find courage to ask for what we need, and how trust in God transforms us even when circumstances seem to contradict his promises.

We then discover how this inner work produces something that others can sense in us: an outward fragrance—the 'aroma of Christ', as it were—that touches those around us, leading us to bear witness to God's love in both word and deed. Finally, we arrive at the cross, where we witness not our own heart work, but see that the transformation of our own hearts is brought about through God's ultimate heart work revealed in the gift of the life of his own Son Jesus Christ on the cross.

As I was writing each chapter, I wanted to give readers an introduction to the rich spiritual tradition of the Church that I first encountered as an undergraduate studying theology in Oxford and which informed my writing. During those formative years, I had the joy and privilege to have been taught by Sister Benedicta Ward SLG, who introduced me to the spiritual writers of the Desert Mothers and Fathers, the writings of St Benedict and St Teresa of Ávila, St John of the Cross, and the English mystics.

Sister Benedicta, knowing I was a native German speaker, encouraged me to explore the writings of the English mystics in their original. I still recall my determined attempts to decode Julian of Norwich's Middle English (which is only a little bit like German). I also vividly remember Sister Benedicta's apologetic announcement at my final exams that if any students wanted to answer questions on St John of the Cross, she was sorry, but the printers had omitted them! Thankfully, I had revised the spiritual writings of St Teresa instead.

I have been working academically with these theologians ever since, both in my sermons, and in the books I write. Just weeks before my accident, my partner Katherine and I had submitted a book chapter on the idea of the 'heart' in German pietist theology in the works of J.S. Bach. In writing this book, I had to learn to put those ideas into practice. At the end of every chapter, I provide a historical perspective, which is meant as encouragement to delve deeper. And at the end of the book, I provide notes and a 'reading list' to help you shape your own theological reflections.

My journey of heart work has been transformational for me, but it has not been easy. There will be times in your own heart work when your heart aches precisely because you've opened it. That was true for me, and it may be so for you. Let me assure you that this is normal and necessary. Just as physical rehabilitation involves pain as atrophied muscles are strengthened and damaged tissues are stretched—and I am most grateful to my physiotherapists for their determined care in setting my own shoulder and muscles to work again—so spiritual heart work involves another set of discomforts: vulnerability, honesty, and change.

God longs to console us when we open ourselves to his grace in prayer. During my recovery, as the pain in my arm and shoulder kept me awake in the silent hours of the night, I found myself holding before God others in pain: the names and faces of people I had met or engaged with that day who, I felt, needed the compassion and help of Christ—including my family and myself. These night-time vigils taught me much about being more compassionate to others and towards myself. Because when we acknowledge our own need for grace, we become more gracious towards others.

A word about anger: as you engage in heart work, you may find yourself experiencing anger at the injustices in our world or the hardened hearts of others. This anger is not contrary to heart work: anger can become purposeful rather than self-destructive. When faced with such anger, pause to ask what God would have you do with this powerful emotion—how might it be channelled into compassionate action rather than reactive outbursts? Heart work can even transform our anger into a force for good.

As we experience anger or witness pain in those around us, we walk a delicate balance, learning to witness the pain of others without taking it into ourselves. The key to this is learning to let go, something I need to remind myself of daily. As I write these words in autumn, I can see the leaves outside the Deanery windows gradually releasing from the trees—they neither cling desperately nor fall prematurely. We, too, can learn to witness to suffering, to respond to pain with appropriate righteous anger or compassionate care, and then to release what is not ours to carry into Christ's care. And then, like the autumn leaves falling to the ground, letting go: trusting that Christ carries all burdens and that God's work continues.

After the journey of Lent comes Easter: the celebration of Christ's resurrection that transforms our understanding of suffering and vulnerability. As Christians, we hold a unique perspective—we know that death has been overcome, and that the risen Jesus carries in his glorified body the scars of his pierced side and hands. These wounds, which he invited Thomas to touch, are not blemishes that he hides but are visible—eternal—signs of the open heart of God. They remind us that our own heart work, our own woundedness, is not erased in resurrection but transformed. The scars remain, but they become signs of our own healing and reminders to us of God's enduring grace.

I hope that this Easter perspective will infuse your own heart work with hope—the assurance that our openness to God, even when painful, leads not to destruction but to new life.

My prayer is that this book will serve as a companion on your own journey of heart work. Whether you're reading this during Lent or at another season of life, I pray that these reflections would help you open your heart to the One who created it; who knows its every crevice, and who longs to dwell there as both guest and host.

The Deanery, Melbourne, Holy Week 2025

How to Use this Book

Each chapter of the book is designed as a weekly devotional: with Scripture readings, reflections on the theme of heart work, theological insights into the Christian tradition, questions for discussion, suggested spiritual practices, and a closing prayer.

The weeks of Lent, and Holy Week, provide an ideal framework for reading this book, either in a group or on your own—both because Lent is traditionally a season of spiritual renewal and inward transformation, and because the book's progression mirrors the Lenten journey towards the cross and resurrection. The final chapter, focused on Good Friday, brings our exploration of heart work to its culmination in the open heart of God revealed on the cross.

However, this book could be used at any other time during the year, as the message of heart work—God's transformative action within us—is relevant to our Christian journey whether we're facing difficulties, supporting others, navigating challenges in society, or seeking deeper communion with God and our fellow believers. You might find different ways to engage with this material depending on your current season of life.

Using this book in groups

Genuine heart work adapts to different contexts and communities. Just as the early church found ways to build community in diverse settings—from urban Jerusalem to rural Galilee, from sophisticated Athens to imperial Rome—the reflections in this book can be tailored to meet people where they are.

This book could be especially meaningful for Lenten study groups, confirmation or baptism preparation classes, church leadership development, or clergy retreats. The emphasis on inward transformation that manifests in outward change speaks to Christians at all stages of their journey.

I originally prepared these reflections as sermons for my Cathedral congregations, but I believe this book would work equally well for ongoing small groups, Bible studies, or youth groups. It could also serve as the framework for an intensive retreat, with each chapter forming a morning or afternoon session. However you meet, each chapter stands as a complete study unit.

I recommend spending time each session engaging deeply with the historical Christian perspectives on the heart and the spiritual traditions that underpin heart work that are included in each chapter.

For groups that appreciate substantial preparation, members could read the entire chapter beforehand and perhaps explore some of the suggested further reading, coming to the discussion fully prepared to work through the questions together.

For groups where extensive reading isn't practical, a leader or group member could present the main points from each chapter. The presenter might use the Scripture readings and main reflections to guide the discussion. When you gather, you could begin by reading the Scripture passages aloud or silently, depending on your group's preferences. Remember that some participants may find certain formats more accessible than others.

Each chapter includes reflection questions to help you explore the week's theme. You can address all the questions, giving each equal time, or focus more deeply on one or two that resonate particularly with your group. At the end of the book I include some suggested questions that cover the entire book, which you may wish to use with Book Groups that only meet once a month, rather than weekly.

I suggest closing each session with prayer. You might read the provided prayer aloud, have everyone read it silently, or offer your own prayers inspired by that week's theme.

Between sessions, participants might place the weekly prayer somewhere visible—on a calendar, pinboard, or refrigerator. Praying this prayer daily until the next meeting can help sustain the individual heart work which you have begun during your gathering.

Using this book as an individual

As an individual reader, you have great flexibility in how you approach this book. You might read through the Scripture readings in sequence, focus on the reflection questions, or pray with the closing prayers.

Perhaps you'll select one chapter that seems particularly relevant to your current spiritual journey and sit with it for an extended time, repeatedly reading and reflecting on how God might be inviting you into deeper heart work. Or you might read the entire book at once, gaining a comprehensive view of Lenten heart work.

This book can also serve as a guide for personal retreat days during Lent. Each chapter could structure a Sunday of prayer and reflection, with the spiritual practices providing concrete ways to engage with that week's theme.

For spiritual directors, chaplains, or clergy, these reflections might offer fresh perspectives for accompanying others in their journey of transformation, providing language and imagery for the sometimes-ineffable experience of God's work in human hearts.

Using this book as a whole church community

Since these reflections originated as sermons, you might use the chapter structure to shape a Lenten preaching series or any season focused on spiritual renewal. The themes would be appropriate for youth ministry with older adolescents (16+) or young adult groups. The reflection questions could inspire your own sermon preparation.

Most churches already include Scripture readings in worship, and you might incorporate this book's Scripture passages into your lectionary. The weekly prayers could inform your intercessions. The historical perspectives on the heart in Christian tradition might enrich adult education programs or study groups running alongside the sermon series.

Some congregations incorporate poetry and contemplative elements in worship, and the prayer activities on the themes of each chapter—from the inward journey to the open heart of God—could inspire creative liturgical expressions throughout Lent.

However you use this book, I hope you find it as inspiring, challenging, and heart-opening as I did when preparing it. May it lead you deeper into the heart work that God desires to accomplish in each of us—the transformation that begins when we let Christ dwell in our hearts and, sustained by his grace, enables us to work as his fellow workers to change our world.

1

The Inward Journey of Lent

Rembrandt Harmenszoon van Rijn (1606-69),
The Return of the Prodigal Son,
Etching, 1636.

SCRIPTURE READINGS

¹² Yet even now, says the Lord,
return to me with all your heart,
with fasting, with weeping, and with mourning;
¹³ rend your hearts and not your clothing.
Return to the Lord, your God,
for he is gracious and merciful,
slow to anger, and abounding in steadfast love,
and relents from punishing.

Joel 2:12-17

As God's fellow workers, we urge you also not to accept the grace of God in vain. ² For he says,
   'At an acceptable time I have listened to you,
   and on a day of salvation I have helped you'.
   See, now is the acceptable time; see, now is the day of salvation! ³ We are putting no obstacle in anyone's way, so that no fault may be found with our ministry, ⁴ but as servants of God we have commended ourselves in every way: through great endurance, in afflictions, hardships, calamities, ⁵ beatings, imprisonments, riots, labours, sleepless nights, hunger; ⁶ by purity, knowledge, patience, kindness, holiness of spirit, genuine love, ⁷ truthful speech, and the power of God; with the weapons of righteousness for the right hand and for the left; ⁸ in honour and dishonour, in ill repute and good repute. We are treated as impostors, and yet are true; ⁹ as unknown, and yet are well known; as dying, and see—we are alive; as punished, and yet not killed; ¹⁰ as sorrowful, yet always rejoicing; as poor, yet making many rich; as having nothing, and yet possessing everything.

2 Corinthians 6:1-10

The Inward Journey of Lent

Thank you for embarking on this Lenten journey of heart work. I wrote this reflection only weeks after my bicycle accident, and I had just reached one of the many small milestones on the way of recovery: my arm was no longer in a sling. No more painful wrestling into my robes and then putting on the sling to protect my arm. There was more: I was allowed to carry the equivalent weight of a cup of tea in my left arm. That enabled me to lead the imposition of ashes on Ash Wednesday, holding the light container with ashes with my 'bad arm' and tracing the ancient sign of ashes on the foreheads of our congregants. That stark symbol—dust to dust, ashes to ashes—serves as a visible reminder: not only of our mortality, but of our profound need for the life that only God can give. As the gritty ash touches our skin, we acknowledge our frailty, our finitude, and our fallenness.

As we set out on our series of reflections, we find ourselves at a threshold. If you are reading this on Ash Wednesday, the season of Lent stretches out before us—forty days of reflection, repentance, and renewal. Of course, you can set aside time for reflection and renewal at any other time of the year. Either way, we are encouraged enter into our own wilderness journeys, like the people of Israel who once wandered forty years in the wilderness. Our promised land is the kingdom of God; resurrection life with Christ forever. And because our journey is to a kingdom that transcends time and place, we orient ourselves not by maps but God's word, and we travel not across the Sinai Peninsula like the people of Israel on their exodus from slavery but in the landscape of our hearts.

In the first reading we consider in this chapter, the prophet Joel speaks to us with urgency: 'Yet even now, says the Lord, return to me with all your heart, with fasting, with weeping, and with mourning' (Joel 2:12). Even now—in the middle of our busy days, in the midst of our complicated lives, amid our successes and failures—God calls us to take stock, to take time, so that we may re-orient our lives towards him.

Notice how Joel describes this return. This is not a casual stop on the way, nor a brief nod by way of acknowledgement, but turning full circle. 'Return with all your heart', the prophet tells us—leaving no room for half-measures or divided loyalties. Such a wholehearted return involves both outward disciplines—'fasting, weeping, and mourning'—and inward transformation. Joel calls us not to ritualistic observance alone, but to a genuine change that begins deep within.

And that is precisely what Lent means. Lent is not primarily about giving up chocolate or coffee, though these disciplines may help shape our journey. Rather, Lent is fundamentally about inner conversion, inner change. Something that happens in secret; deep inside us. The outward practices are valuable precisely because they can support and nurture our inward renewal, because they can create space in our cluttered lives for God's transforming presence.

Rending Hearts, Not Garments

The prophet Joel continues with a striking image: 'Rend your hearts and not your clothing', Joel tells us (Joel 2:13). In ancient times, tearing one's garments was a gesture of profound grief or distress—a visible, public display of emotion. But Joel suggests that such external demonstrations miss the point if they aren't accompanied by a deeper rending. The tearing open of our hearts.

What does it mean to 'rend our hearts'? It means allowing the protective layers that we have built around ourselves—layers of self-justification, pride, and denial—to be torn away, exposing our true selves to God's gaze in the expectation that God will grant us his grace. It means becoming vulnerable before the One who sees all and knows all, and yet loves us so completely that he gifts us the grace to return to him.

This opening to God's gaze and grace is what the psalmist prayed for: 'Create in me a clean heart, O God, and renew a right spirit within me' (Psalm 51:10). The psalmist recognises that true transformation is

God's work *within us*, and not *our* work *for* God. We are not able, in our own strength, to cleanse our own hearts, or renew our own spirits. We can only open ourselves to God, who promises renewal at the most profound level.

From Hard Work to Heart Work

We live in a world that values hard work. Many cultures pride themselves on being places of industry and accomplishment. Many of us move through workplaces where productivity and output are constantly measured by KPIs or, for church workers, Mission Objectives. Our society celebrates the visible fruits of labour—promotions earned, deals negotiated, targets met. Hard work is about what we can achieve through our own strength, our own determination. It's about the outcomes that others can see and applaud.

But Lent calls us to a different kind of effort. Not *hard* work, but *heart* work.

Heart surgery remains one of the most complex and delicate medical procedures we perform. When surgeons work on a heart, they temporarily have to stop it, diverting its life-sustaining function to machines. The chest has to be opened, exposing our most vital organ to intervention. Following such profound invasion, recovery is not immediate—it requires weeks of careful management, months of rehabilitation, and a lifetime of attention to cardiac health.

This medical reality offers a good analogy for the heart work of spiritual renewal. The work God does in our hearts is no less intricate, no less profound, no less intimidating. It requires an opening of ourselves to divine intervention—allowing God to access the very core of our being.

While hard work focuses on external achievements that are often temporary, heart work addresses the eternal. Hard work may bring us worldly success; heart work brings us closer to God. Hard work exhausts our resources; heart work renews them. Hard work is what we do for ourselves and others; heart work is what we allow God to do within us.

The Inner Work of Transformation

God's work of transformation may go entirely unseen, but it does change us at the deepest level of our being. This is heart work—the difficult, unseen, and sometimes painful process of allowing God to rework us from the inside out. And like medical rehabilitation after an injury or surgery, spiritual renewal is not instantaneous but demands our continued participation in the healing process.

In the reading from Second Corinthians we consider in this chapter, St Paul encourages us to open ourselves to God's grace: we are not to accept God's grace in vain but need to recognise that 'now is the acceptable time; now is the day of salvation' (2 Corinthians 6:1-2). Paul not only tells us to take a leap of faith, but he points to his own life story in making sense of the profound inner transformation that occurs when we surrender our hearts to God.

For the world, our transformation in Christ may look like a failure: as Christ died a lonely death on a forlorn cross outside the walls of his faith community. Similarly, our own allegiance to him, our opening our hearts to him, may be seen as a failure. By the standards of hard work—of visible achievement and worldly success—the Christian life often appears foolish. Paul knows that we may be treated as impostors, yet are true; as unknown, yet well-known; as dying, yet alive; as sorrowful, yet always rejoicing (2 Corinthians 6:8-10).

But in God's eye, our surrender to him, our opening of our hearts, is the greatest victory. It is the beginning of our life as disciples. Just as Christ's apparent defeat on the cross became the moment of ultimate triumph, so our own vulnerability before God may transform our weakness into strength, our brokenness into wholeness, our sorrow into joy.

That's why Paul takes such care to remind us that the outward circumstances of our lives—whether marked by affliction, hardship, or calamity—cannot prevent the inner renewal that God offers. Hard work may be thwarted by circumstance; heart work transcends it. Indeed, it is often in moments of greatest difficulty—when our hard work seems most futile—that our hearts are most open to God's healing. It's often in those moments when our carefully constructed façades crack, when our own strength fails us, that God's grace can enter most deeply to begin the work of healing.

The God who waits

As we begin this spiritual journey together, remember that the God who seeks to rework us, the God to whom we return is, as Joel reminds us, 'gracious and merciful, slow to anger, and abounding in steadfast love' (Joel 2:13). When we turn to God, we turn to the Heavenly Father who already faces us: who has been looking out for us, and is waiting for our return. When we walk towards him, Jesus tells us in one of his best-known stories—that of the Lost or Prodigal Son—he will run to meet us on our way and bring us home; he will embrace us and bless us.

On our journey together, we are invited to move beyond hard work to heart work. To set aside time each day for that inner work of renewal. To come before God with honesty and vulnerability, asking him for the gift of a heart made clean and a spirit renewed.

May this season be for you a time of genuine heart work. May we experience God's healing and renewal at the very core of our being, that we might live more fully as disciples of the One who gave his life so that we may have life in abundance. And may we arrive at the end of our journey—our spiritual Easter—with hearts more open, more loving, more centred on the heart of Christ himself.

In the next chapter, we'll explore how this inward heart work relates to faith and how Christ has fulfilled the law on our behalf, freeing us to live from grace rather than works.

WORKING DEEPER

The Heart in Christian Tradition

Throughout Christian history, the heart has been understood as far more than a physical organ. In biblical understanding, the heart is the centre of the whole person—the seat of thought, emotion, will, and spiritual life. When Scripture speaks of the heart, it refers to our deepest self, the core of our being where our most fundamental commitments and orientations are formed.

St Augustine of Hippo, writing in the late fourth and early fifth centuries, reflected deeply on the restless heart that can find no peace until it rests in God. He understood that the human heart is made for God and continually seeks return to its source. His famous prayer captures this reality: 'You have made us for yourself, O Lord, and our hearts are restless until they rest in you' (*Confessions*).

For St Benedict of Nursia, the founder of Western monasticism, heart work was practiced through the rhythms of *ora et labora* (prayer and work). The Benedictine tradition emphasises attentiveness and intentionality in all things, thus creating space in daily life for God's transformative presence.

In the Eastern Orthodox tradition, the Jesus Prayer— 'Lord Jesus Christ, Son of God, have mercy on me, a sinner'—is repeated as a way of centring our hearts on Christ. This practice of the 'prayer of the heart' seeks to unite the mind and heart in continuous awareness of God's presence.

The medieval mystic St Julian of Norwich wrote of God's dwelling in the heart, where divine love transforms human suffering into joy. For Dame Julian, heart work meant trusting God's goodness even amid life's greatest pains (*Revelations of Divine Love*).

In our own time, Henri Nouwen described the heart as 'the place where we are most ourselves, where we are most human, most vulnerable, most sensitive, most caring' (*Life of the Beloved*). Lenten heart work invites us to this vulnerable centre where authentic transformation can occur.

Reflection Questions

1. The prophet Joel calls us to 'return to God with all your heart'. What barriers or protective layers might you need to remove to turn more fully towards God this Lent?

2. When have you experienced the difference between 'hard work' (external achievements) and 'heart work' (internal transformation)? How did each affect you differently?

3. Paul describes followers of Christ as being 'treated as impostors, yet true; as unknown, yet well-known; as dying, yet alive; as sorrowful, yet always rejoicing'. Which of these paradoxes resonates most with your own experience of faith? Why?

4. The psalmist prays, 'Create in me a clean heart, O God' (Psalm 51:10). What aspects of your heart would you like God to cleanse or renew during this Lenten season?

5. How might you create space in your daily life for God's transformative work in your heart?

Spiritual Practices for the Week

1. **Heart Awareness**: Each day this week, spend a few minutes in silence with your hand over your heart. As you feel your heartbeat, reflect on this being the place where God seeks to dwell and work. Simply be present to God in this awareness.

2. Rending Prayer: Write down on a piece of paper something you've been holding back from God—a fear, a doubt, a habitual sin. Tear the paper as a physical symbol of 'rending your heart' and opening yourself to God's grace. Then pray for God's healing presence in this area of your life.

3. Simplicity Fast: Choose one day this week to fast from busy-ness and productivity. Set aside your to-do list and practice being rather than doing. Notice how this creates space for God's presence in your heart.

Closing Prayer

Gracious and merciful God, you call us to return with all our hearts: we come before you at the beginning of this spiritual journey.

Help us to rend our hearts and not merely our garments, to move beyond outward observance to inward transformation.

Lord, have mercy: *Lord, have mercy.*

Create in us clean hearts, O God, and renew right spirits within us. Give us courage to let you access the very core of our being, to allow your healing grace to touch those places we have kept hidden even from ourselves.

Christ, have mercy: *Christ, have mercy.*

As we set aside time for heart work in these forty days, may we experience the deep renewal that only you can bring.

Lord, have mercy: *Lord, have mercy.*

2

From Law to Faith

Overleaf

Hans Baldung Grien (1484-1545),
The Conversion of Paul,
Woodcut, 1514.

SCRIPTURE READINGS

[11] Surely, this commandment that I am commanding you today is not too hard for you, nor is it too far away. [12] It is not in heaven, that you should say, 'Who will go up to heaven for us, and get it for us so that we may hear it and observe it?' [13] Neither is it beyond the sea, that you should say, 'Who will cross to the other side of the sea for us, and get it for us so that we may hear it and observe it?' [14] No, the word is very near to you; it is in your mouth and in your heart for you to observe.

Deuteronomy 30:11-14

[4] Christ is the end of the law so that there may be righteousness for everyone who believes. [5] Moses writes concerning the righteousness that comes from the law, that 'the person who does these things will live by them'. [6] But the righteousness that comes from faith says, 'Do not say in your heart, "Who will ascend into heaven?"' (that is, to bring Christ down) [7] or "Who will descend into the abyss?"' (that is, to bring Christ up from the dead). [8] But what does it say?

'The word is near you,
   on your lips and in your heart'.

Romans 10:4-13

In the previous chapter, we began our spiritual journey by reflecting on 'heart work'—the inward transformation that God seeks to bring about in each of us. We contrasted 'heart work' with the 'hard work' of outward religious observance and the targets and achievements celebrated by our society. In this chapter we are invited to explore this theme further, and to delve more deeply into seeing how, when we let God work in our hearts, we are changed; how God brings about righteousness and salvation. In the reading from St Paul's Letter to the Romans we consider in this chapter, Paul sets out how close God seeks to come to us when we let him.

Paul's letter to the Romans is addressed to a community of Jewish and Gentile Christians—people with very different understandings of how individuals should relate to God. For Jewish believers, the law of Moses had been the path to righteousness for generations. For Gentile converts, this was alien territory. The message of Paul to both groups is revolutionary: 'Christ is the end of the law so that there may be righteousness for everyone who believes' (Romans 10:4).

What happens when the law ends?

What does Paul mean when he declares that 'Christ is the end of the law'? The Greek word Paul uses—*télos*—carries a number of meanings. The word can mean either 'termination' or 'conclusion', but it can also mean 'goal' or 'fulfilment'. In Jesus Christ, then, God's law reaches both its culmination and its conclusion; in Christ, God fulfils his law.

For centuries, the people of God had striven to attain righteousness by their meticulous obedience to the law. Paul reminds us how Moses, in Leviticus 18, had told the people of Israel: 'Those who do these things'—God's laws that Moses gave the people—'will live by them' (Romans 10:5, citing Leviticus 18:5). Such an approach to righteousness required hard work—constant vigilance, scrupulous attention to detail, rigorous self-discipline.

The path of hard work is a path many believers still instinctively follow. We think that if we only try harder, pray longer, study more deeply, give more generously, or serve more sacrificially, we will somehow earn God's approval. When we engage in spiritual 'hard work'—we attempt to achieve salvation through our own efforts. And inevitably, we find ourselves exhausted, discouraged, and still falling short of what God has set out in his laws.

That's where Paul's message is so liberating. He tells the Jewish and Gentile followers of Jesus in Rome that Christ has put an end to this futile struggle. Christ has fulfilled the law's demands on our behalf. This changes everything about how we relate to God. The hard work that you and I could never complete has already been accomplished in him. On the cross, all was accomplished. When Christ breathes his last, he exclaims, *'tetélestai'*—'It is finished'. The law is fulfilled. Hard work is accomplished, so that heart work may begin. And that work begins when you and I enter into the path of discipleship: by taking up our cross daily, and following Jesus.

Or to use the language of Paul's letter to the Romans: heart work begins when we open our own hearts to God and his word.

The Word Near Us

God's word is never far from us, Paul assures the Romans. And again he quotes Moses; this time from Deuteronomy 30. He frames his argument by way of a rhetorical question: 'Do not say in your heart, "Who will ascend into heaven?"' (Romans 10:6), he asks his Roman readers. In its original context, Moses was telling the Israelites that God's commandment 'is not too difficult for you or beyond your reach. It is not in heaven, so that you have to ask, "Who will ascend into heaven to get it and proclaim it to us?"' (Deuteronomy 30:11-12). Moses made clear that God's word was much nearer than heaven, or the abyss. It was right there; fully accessible to God's people.

And now Paul takes the words of Moses, spoken at the end of the forty-year sojourn through the desert on the way to the Promised Land, to speak of the work of Jesus Christ. We don't need to ascend to heaven ourselves to bring Christ down or descend to the depths to bring him up from the dead. God has already done the impossible for us. The Incarnation has happened: Christ was made flesh and born a human child laid in a manger. The resurrection is accomplished: Christ truly died and was raised from the dead. God's living word is much closer to us than heaven and hell—it's in our mouths and in our hearts.

Hard Work vs. Heart Work

This is what heart work is about. Rather than do the hard work of trying to move heaven and earth, and possibly plunge hell as well in order to gain Christ, we need to look inside us.

Hard work says: 'I must work harder to reach God'.

Heart work, on the other hand, knows that God has already reached down to us. Hard work is based on our own achievements; heart work is based on God choosing to come close to us.

The heart surgeon doesn't ask the patient to perform their own operation. That would be impossible. Instead, it's the surgeon who undertakes the complex, delicate work of repair. Our role as patients is to trust in the expertise and skill and then to participate actively in the rehab process. While the surgeon does the essential healing, our cooperation in rehabilitation is crucial for full recovery. In the same way, God has already accomplished the work of our salvation. Our role is to trust in his salvation and grace, and then live out of the strength, and into the power, of the healing he provides.

When I wrote this reflection, I had just started hydrotherapy. I loved being back in the pool. My arm felt so light. Supported by the buoyancy of the water, I made my first lateral exercises to train the mobility of my shoulder. One of the things I had found particularly frustrating and painful had been reaching behind my back—something most people do quite naturally when we dress. My first attempts were very challenging—I was unable to force the movement through sheer determination. In the pool, my hydro-therapist Tom taught me to work with the buoyancy of the water, relaxing into the movement, rather than fight my limitations. For me, accepting my current limitations while working with Tom towards healing was a good reminder of the way in which God's grace seeks to work in our lives. The buoyancy of the water helping me regain greater movement in my broken arm was a bit like God helping our movement through life by grace.

Faith in Heart and Mouth

At the heart of Paul's letter to the Romans stands this affirmation: 'If you confess with your mouth, "Jesus is Lord", and believe in your heart that God raised him from the dead, you will be saved. For it is with your heart that you believe and are justified, and it is with your mouth that you confess and are saved' (Romans 10:9-10). Paul here highlights both the inward and outward dimensions of our faith. Believing is something internal, it's a reality that is rooted in our hearts. But true faith doesn't remain private—it needs to find expression in public confession and public service.

In the first chapter, we reflected on the prophet Joel's call to 'rend your hearts and not your garments' in response to God's invitation to turn to him (Joel 2:13). We were invited to interior conversion, not outward ritual. Now, Paul makes an important further connection. The rent heart—the heart that is opened to God's grace—naturally leads to confession. The heart that has been transformed by God's work can't help but speak, something we will consider more fully in chapter 6.

That is a pattern we can recognise throughout Scripture. Isaiah cried, 'Woe is me!' when he beheld God's holiness, but on encountering the transformational power of God we call 'grace' he then declared: 'Here am I, send me!' (Isaiah 6:5, 8). In the same way at the beginning of his own journey with Jesus, Peter fell at his knees trying to turn Jesus away: 'Go away from me, Lord, for I am a sinful man', he exclaimed. But later, as he encountered more and more of the grace-filled acts and teachings of Jesus, he boldly confessed him as 'the Christ, the Son of the living God' (Luke 5:8, 9:20). Heart work always manifests in outward expression. The heart that has experienced God's grace cannot do other than become a heart that confesses God's goodness.

Grace for All

You may say to yourself: 'I can see how this may be true for the heroes of faith: Isaiah was a powerful prophet, and Peter the rock on which the church is built. But I am not a powerful prophet, or the rock on which the church rests'. Well, Paul has good news for us. The same grace that is at work in the heroes of faith like Isaiah and Peter is also at work in each one of us. There is no essential difference. All are included: regardless of background, even regardless of past experience or action. As Paul explains in his letter to the Romans: 'For there is no difference between Jew and Gentile—the same Lord is Lord of all and richly blesses all who call on him, for "Everyone who calls on the name of the Lord will be saved".' (Romans 10:12-13). That is indeed good news: heart work is open to all.

Where the path of hard work always creates distinctions, heart work is accessible to all. Where hard work distinguishes between those who achieve more and those who achieve less, between experts and novices, between the disciplined and the struggling, the path of grace eliminates these distinctions. The same Lord is Lord of all, and he responds with equal generosity to all who call on him, Paul knows.

This is perhaps the most revolutionary aspect of Paul's message. In a world that—then and now—is divided by ethnicity, culture, social status, and religious background, Paul proclaims a level playing field.

At the foot of the cross, the ground is level. Because Christ took down all division into himself at the cross, and broke all barriers by letting himself be broken, we may approach him with confidence—confidence that each one of us may approach and ask for grace. Because each one of us, regardless of our background or achievements, stands in need of God's grace. And we are assured that each one of us, who calls on our loving God in faith, will receive the same generous response.

Heart work isn't reserved for church leaders, biblical heroes, or spiritual giants. It's the everyday transformation that happens in ordinary lives—the office worker who prays for colleagues, the parent who demonstrates forgiveness to their children, the student who stands for justice among peers. Where God's word dwells in our hearts, each of us can become a unique expression of his grace, regardless of title or position. The beauty of Paul's message is that the same Lord richly blesses all who call on him—from spiritual leaders to first-time seekers, from lifelong believers to those who are just beginning their journeys of faith.

Living out of Grace, Not Works

As we continue our spiritual journey, we are invited to move deeper into heart work—to allow God's word to dwell richly within us, transforming us from the inside out. We're called to set aside the exhausting path of hard work, of striving to earn what can only be received as gift.

As we travel with Christ this season, may we come to realise more deeply that he has already accomplished what we could not do. Christ has fulfilled the law's demands. He has made God's saving presence accessible to us. He has opened the way for all people to experience God's grace.

Our response to such good news is faith. We are called to believe in our hearts and confess with our mouths. Our response is to receive the word that is near us—not distant or inaccessible, but as close as our own heartbeat. Our calling is to open our hearts wide to God's grace and to live into the reality of God's transforming love, so freely gifted to us.

As we journey together, let us make time to allow God to continue the heart work he has begun in us. May we set aside our striving and instead rest in his finished work. May we open our hearts to the word that is near us and allow that word to transform us from inside out. As we journey together, may we grow in our understanding of who Jesus is and what he has done, so that our confession becomes not just words on our lips but the deepest conviction of our hearts.

Having seen how God's word is made accessible to our hearts through Christ, we'll next explore another dimension of heart work: finding the courage to ask God for what we truly need.

WORKING DEEPER

From Law to Grace in Christian Thought

The tension between law and grace has been a recurring theme throughout Christian history. Early Church Fathers like Justin Martyr and Irenaeus wrestled with how to understand the relationship between the Mosaic Law and the gospel of Christ. Irenaeus described the Law as a pedagogue—a guardian or tutor—that prepared humanity for the revelation of Christ.

St Augustine developed a profound theology of grace that emphasised its gratuitous nature. Against Pelagius, who taught that humans could achieve righteousness through proper use of their God-given capacities, Augustine insisted that divine grace was not merely assistance for human effort but the very source of our ability to respond to God at all. His famous prayer, 'Command what you will, and give what you command', captures this understanding of the primacy of grace (*Confessions*).

The medieval church saw various attempts to articulate the relationship between human effort and divine grace. St Thomas Aquinas taught that grace builds on nature rather than destroying it—grace perfects what is already good in creation rather than negating it entirely.

The Protestant Reformation brought renewed emphasis on the themes Paul addresses in Romans. Martin Luther's breakthrough insight that righteousness comes through faith alone (*sola fide*) rather than through works rediscovered the heart of Paul's message. Luther described this as a 'happy exchange' (*fröhlicher Wechsel*) whereby Christ takes our sin and gives us his righteousness.

In more recent times, theologians like Karl Barth have emphasised that grace precedes even our faith response—God's 'yes' to humanity in Christ comes before our 'yes' to God. Meanwhile, the ecumenical movement has helped both Catholic and Protestant Christians recognise their common ground in affirming that salvation comes by grace through faith rather than through works of the law.

The Eastern Orthodox tradition offers another perspective through its emphasis on *theosis* or deification—the gradual transformation of the believer through participation in divine grace. St Athanasius expressed this succinctly: 'God became human so that humans might become divine' (*On the Incarnation*). This tradition reminds us that heart work is ultimately about being conformed to the image of Christ through the indwelling presence of the Holy Spirit.

Reflection Questions

1. When have you found yourself trying to 'earn' God's approval through your own efforts? How did this approach affect your relationship with God?

2. Paul writes that 'Christ is the end (*télos*) of the law'. How does understanding Christ as both the fulfilment and conclusion of the law change your perspective on spiritual disciplines and practices?

3. The passage emphasises that God's word is 'near you, in your mouth and in your heart'. When have you experienced God's presence as close rather than distant? What helped you recognise this nearness?

4. 'If you confess with your mouth ... and believe in your heart ... you will be saved'. How do the internal (heart) and external (mouth) aspects of faith work together in your spiritual life? Is one easier for you than the other?

5. Paul emphasises that the same Lord is 'Lord of all and richly blesses all who call on him'. How might this understanding of God's impartiality challenge the way we view others who are different from us?

Spiritual Practices for the Week

1. Heart Listening: Set aside 15 minutes each day this week to listen to God's word in your heart. Choose a short Scripture passage (perhaps Romans 10:9-10), read it slowly, and then sit in silence, paying attention to what stirs within you. Remember, God's word is not far away but already near you.

2. Grace Awareness: Throughout each day, notice moments when you slip into 'earning' mode—trying to prove your worth or gain approval. When you catch yourself, pause and remember Paul's words that salvation comes through faith, not works. Take a deep breath and mentally repeat, 'Christ has fulfilled the law; I am saved by grace through faith'.

3. Confession Practice: Following Paul's emphasis on both believing in the heart and confessing with the mouth, choose a simple affirmation of faith that resonates with you (such as 'Jesus is Lord' or 'Christ has died, Christ is risen, Christ will come again'). Speak it aloud daily—not as a formula, but as a way of allowing your internal belief to find external expression.

Closing Prayer

Gracious God, source of all goodness, we thank you that in Christ you have accomplished what we could never achieve through our own efforts. Thank you that your word is not distant or inaccessible, but near us—in our mouths and in our hearts.

Lord in your mercy: *hear our prayer.*

Forgive us for the times we have tried to earn your love through our religious performances or moral achievements. We rest now in the finished work of Christ, who is the fulfilment of the law and the perfecter of our faith.

Lord in your mercy: *hear our prayer.*

Open our hearts to receive your grace anew. May we believe deeply and confess boldly that Jesus is Lord, the one who lived, died, and rose again for us. And through this faith, may we experience the righteousness that comes not from our striving but from your generous gift.

Lord in your mercy: *hear our prayer.*

As we continue our spiritual journey, help us to set aside the exhausting path of hard work and embrace the transformative way of heart work. May Jesus, your living word dwell richly within us, changing us from the inside out. In his name we pray. *Amen.*

3

The Courage to Ask

Lucas van Leyden (1489/1494-1533),
Queen Esther before Ahasuerus,
Engraving, 1518.

SCRIPTURE READINGS

Esther prayed to the Lord God of Israel, and said: 'O my Lord, you only are our king; help me, who am alone and have no helper but you, [4] for my danger is in my hand. [5] Ever since I was born I have heard in the tribe of my family that you, O Lord, took Israel out of all the nations, and our ancestors from among all their forebears, for an everlasting inheritance, and that you did for them all that you promised. [6] And now we have sinned before you, and you have handed us over to our enemies [7] because we glorified their gods. You are righteous, O Lord! [8] And now they are not satisfied that we are in bitter slavery, but they have covenanted with their idols [9] to abolish what your mouth has ordained, and to destroy your inheritance, to stop the mouths of those who praise you and to quench your altar and the glory of your house, [10] to open the mouths of the nations for the praise of vain idols, and to magnify forever a mortal king.

[11] 'O Lord, do not surrender your sceptre to what has no being; and do not let them laugh at our downfall; but turn their plan against them, and make an example of him who began this against us. [12] Remember, O Lord; make yourself known in this time of our affliction, and give me courage, O King of the gods and Master of all dominion! [13] Put eloquent speech in my mouth before the lion, and turn his heart to hate the man who is fighting against us, so that there may be an end of him and those who agree with him. [14] But save us by your hand, and help me, who am alone and have no helper but you, O Lord'.

Greek Additions to Esther 14:3-14

[7] Jesus said to them: 'Ask, and it will be given you; search, and you will find; knock, and the door will be opened for you. [8] For everyone who asks receives, and everyone who searches finds, and for everyone who knocks, the door will be opened. [9] Is there anyone among you who, if your child asks for bread, will give a stone? [10] Or if the child asks for

a fish, will give a snake? ¹¹ If you then, who are evil, know how to give good gifts to your children, how much more will your Father in heaven give good things to those who ask him! ¹² In everything do to others as you would have them do to you; for this is the law and the prophets'.

Matthew 7:7-12

In the previous two chapters, we have been reflecting together on what we've called 'heart work'—the inward transformation that God seeks to bring about in each of us. We began by contrasting 'heart work' with 'hard work', noting how God calls us not to outward religious observance but to inward renewal. Then we explored how Christ has ended our futile attempts to achieve righteousness through our own efforts, instead making God's word accessible to our hearts. In this chapter, we turn to another dimension of heart work: the courage to ask.

A Queen's Desperate Prayer

In the first Scripture reading we consider in this chapter, from a less frequently read part of the Scriptures, we read a desperate prayer of a fearful Queen. Queen Esther was the Jewish consort of King Ahasuerus, the 'Lion of Persia'. The realm's Grand Vizier, Haman, plotted the extermination of all Jewish people, and Esther decided to intercede for them. Breaking court protocol at risk of her life, she approaches her husband to plead for her people. In this moment of extreme vulnerability, she turns to God with these words: 'O my Lord, you only are our king; help me, who am alone and have no helper but you, for my danger is in my hand' (Greek Esther, 14:3).

Esther's prayer is heart work at its most unabashed. Without any attempt to appear more worthy than she feels, or more spiritual than she is, she speaks her heart, and tells God of her grave anxiety. Esther lays bare her fear and her need for help before God. 'Help me', she prays. 'I am alone and have no helper but you'.

Having asked God for help and, having reminded God of his obligation to the people he has chosen, she then makes her petition. And what is the substance of her prayer; what is it that she asks for? Courage. 'Give me courage', she pleads, 'and put eloquent speech in my mouth' (Greek Esther 14:13). Esther has recognised that what she needs most is not physical protection or a miraculous divine intervention in the crisis that faces her and her fellow-Jews, but the courage and the inner strength to act faithfully so that she may intercede successfully on their behalf.

This is heart work—the recognition that our deepest needs are not necessarily external but internal. What Esther requires is not a change in her circumstances but a change in her own heart. She knows she needs the courage to speak persuasively, advocate for her people, and risk her life for something greater than herself, and so she opens her heart to God, and asks him to put his words in her heart, so that she may speak with his authority: 'O Lord, do not surrender your sceptre to what has no being', she prays; 'but make yourself known in our affliction' (Greek Esther 14:11). And how would God make himself known? By giving his servant Esther great courage.

If you haven't read the story of Esther recently, the effect of her prayer for courage was remarkable. Esther did approach her husband, King Ahasuerus. She spoke boldly of the plans his Grand Vizier had to exterminate her people. And so, the hatred of Haman for God's people turned into the hatred of Ahasuerus in his unfaithful second-in-command. The would-be executor of Jews is executed himself, and the Jewish people are restored to their rightful place in society. The people first to hear God's call continue to tell this story on Purim—a feast Jews celebrate to this day as summer gives way to autumn in the Southern hemisphere (and as winter ends and spring begins in the Northern)—to remind themselves of the story of the Queen who prayed for courage to ask for God's help in trouble.

Jesus on Asking

Four centuries after the story of Esther was written, Jesus preached about how God hears and answers prayer. In the reading from Matthew's Gospel we consider in this chapter, Jesus invites his hearers to adopt the same posture of courageous asking that was Esther's: 'Ask, and it will be given to you; search, and you will find; knock, and the door will be opened for you', he tells (Matthew 7:7). Have courage to ask, and you will be listened to, Jesus tells.

Jesus here encourages a persistent, expectant approach to prayer. This is not a passive waiting for answers, but an active seeking. Such an approach to prayer requires the courage to articulate our deepest needs, to admit that we do not have all that we require, to acknowledge our dependence on God and others. It requires heart work: our willingness to open our hearts to God, to declare our dependence on him, and to ask him for help.

'Lord, help me' is the essence of that prayer. It is interesting that, unlike the first reading we considered, in which the author records in detail the prayer of Esther, Jesus does not report which words the petitioners used. He only describes their actions: ask, search and knock. Because it is based on persistence, rather than proficiency, this kind of asking often runs counter to our natural inclinations. Most people prefer to project self-sufficiency. We hesitate to admit need or vulnerability, because we fear being seen as inadequate or unprepared.

The Courage of Vulnerability

Eight weeks before I wrote this reflection, I had just come off my bike and broken my upper arm. As I picked myself up with bloody scrapes, the person who'd caused the accident asked, 'Are you all right?' I answered, through pain-clenched teeth, 'I'm fine'. I was not. The broken arm required twice-weekly physiotherapy for more than three months. But I preferred not to be fussed over and instead tried to help myself; I preferred hard and painful work rather than admitting my vulnerability and literal brokenness. I chose the route of hard work rather than heart work.

Think about how often we respond to questions about our wellbeing with a quick 'I'm fine' even when we're anything but fine. When we're injured, ill, or struggling, we often prefer not to be fussed over, and instead try to help ourselves; we prefer hard and painful work, rather than admitting our vulnerability and brokenness. But the heart work that this journey invites us to take on requires exactly this kind of vulnerability—the courage to acknowledge our limitations, to have the courage to ask for help.

In the weeks that followed my accident, I had to learn this lesson repeatedly, whether accepting assistance with simple tasks or acknowledging my need for professional medical care. Each moment of vulnerability became an opportunity to experience grace: the grace of those who helped me, the grace of regaining strength and movement. This is what can happen in our spiritual lives too, when we finally admit we cannot heal ourselves and open our hearts to receive help—both from God and from the people God places in our lives.

Bonhoeffer's Prayer

The German pastor Dietrich Bonhoeffer, whose eightieth anniversary of martyrdom fell in April 2025, knew about the importance of heart work. After his arrest for involvement in the plot against Hitler, he was placed in solitary confinement. In his prison cell in Berlin-Tegel he wrote a series of poems and prayers. *Morning Prayer* was written in November 1943, eighteen months before his death.

In the darkest of circumstances—alone in a prison cell, facing an uncertain future—Bonhoeffer does not pretend to have the strength he lacks. Instead, he courageously acknowledges his need: 'I cannot do it alone', he prays. Just as Esther laid bare her fear and vulnerability before God, Bonhoeffer admits his own darkness, loneliness, timidity, anxiety, and bitterness. At every point of his poem, he confesses his own urgent need trusting in God's sufficiency:

> God, I cry to you in the early morning,
> help me to pray and to gather my thoughts;
> I cannot do it alone.
> It is dark inside me, but with you is the light.
> I am lonely, but you do not leave me.
>
> I am timid, but with you is my help.
> I am anxious, but with you is peace.
> There is bitterness inside me, but with you is patience.
> I do not understand your ways,
> but you know the right way for me.

What makes his prayer so powerful is that it comes from a man of remarkable courage and conviction. Bonhoeffer was not weak—he had risked his life to stand against the evils of Nazism. Yet he understood that true strength lay not in self-sufficiency but in acknowledging our dependence on God. In prison, stripped of most external supports, Bonhoeffer came to know what Queen Esther had also experienced: that in our moments of greatest vulnerability, we cannot muster our own courage through hard work, but through the heart work of opening ourselves to receive courage from God. Though our circumstances may differ greatly from Bonhoeffer's prison cell, we all face moments when we must admit our inability to continue alone.

From Personal to Communal Prayer

For both Bonhoeffer and Queen Esther, the courage to ask God for help was not merely an individual virtue. It's a corporate one—something we practice together as a community. That's why Esther frames her prayer in communal language: 'We have sinned before you ... *our* enemies ... *they* are not satisfied that we are in bitter slavery', she prays to God on behalf of her people (Greek Esther 14:6).

In his *Morning Prayer*, Bonhoeffer likewise prays for strength alongside other children of God:

> Let me now receive from your hand,
> what is hard.
> You will not lay upon me
> More than I can bear.
> For your children you let all things
> Serve for the best.

This willingness to accept both what is good and what is hard from God's hands lies at the heart of courageous corporate prayer.

In intense personal danger, Esther knows that she is part of a larger whole. Her courage to ask is inextricably tied to her identity as a member of God's chosen people. For Esther individual faith was no different to her communal responsibility.

The same held true for Bonhoeffer. Even in isolation in prison, he knew that he belonged to a company of believers that suffered hardships—within and outside the prison walls. For both, bearing the burden of courageous asking meant accepting both what is good and what is hard from God's hands; it meant asking for themselves and, in the strength that God provides, giving of their own—however little—to others.

Asking and Giving

Jesus' teaching about prayer we considered leads directly to what we have come to know as the Golden Rule: 'In everything do to others as you would have them do to you; for this is the law and the prophets' (Matthew 7:12). When he compiled his Gospel, Matthew purposefully made that link: because the courage to ask and the generosity to give out of the strength of what we have received are two sides of the same coin. As we open ourselves to receive from God, we become more able to give to others. As we experience God's generous response to our asking, we are enabled to become more generous in our response to the needs of others.

Heart work, then, involves both the courage to ask and the generosity to give. It requires us to be vulnerable before God and responsive towards others. It calls us to recognise our own need and to honour the needs of those around us.

We may not need to intercede before kings like Esther or stand against Nazi dictators like Bonhoeffer. But in our daily lives, we all will encounter moments that call for the same courage they had. Perhaps in families, where admitting vulnerability can be most difficult. Perhaps in workplaces, where we fear appearing incompetent. Perhaps in our neighbourhoods or wider communities, where we see needs that require us to speak up on behalf of others. And certainly, in our relationship with God, where we may feel we should have our spiritual lives more 'together' before we open our mouths to pray.

As we continue our journey, may we cultivate the courage to ask—to approach God with our genuine needs, not disguising or diminishing them out of pride or fear. May we trust, as Esther and Bonhoeffer did, that God hears and responds to our prayers by strengthening our hearts, and may our experience of God's grace, patience, and generous response make us more gracious, patient, and generous towards others.

With the courage to ask established in our hearts, in the next chapter we'll turn to how trust in God transforms us, even when circumstances seem to contradict his promises.

WORKING DEEPER

Prayer as Courage in Christian Tradition

Throughout Christian history, the courage to ask in prayer has been understood as an essential aspect of faith. The Desert Fathers and Mothers of the fourth and fifth centuries—some of the earliest Christian monastics—spoke of prayer as a form of spiritual combat requiring both vulnerability and fortitude. Abba Arsenius taught, 'If we seek God, he will show himself to us, and if we keep him, he will remain with us' (*The Sayings of the Desert Fathers*).

Julian of Norwich, the fourteenth-century English mystic, wrote extensively about prayer during a time of plague and social upheaval. Despite witnessing immense suffering, she insisted on the availability of God: 'Prayer fastens the soul to God and makes it one with his will, through the deep and wide working of the Holy Spirit', she wrote, and described prayer as an act of opening ourselves to the divine presence that is already within us, waiting to be acknowledged (*Revelations of Divine Love*).

St Teresa of Ávila, the sixteenth-century Spanish mystic and reformer, taught that genuine prayer begins with self-knowledge—a courageous acknowledgement of our true condition before God. For Teresa, the courage to ask stemmed from recognising that God already knows our needs better than we do ourselves: 'Let nothing disturb you, let nothing frighten you', she wrote. 'All things pass away: God never changes. Patience obtains all things. Whoever has God lacks nothing; God alone suffices' ('St Teresa's Bookmark'; found in her breviary after her death).

The Reformed tradition, following John Calvin, emphasised that prayer is not primarily about changing God's mind but about aligning ourselves with God's purposes. The courage to ask is ultimately about trusting God's sovereignty and goodness rather than imposing our will. As Calvin wrote, 'prayer is not so much for God's sake as for our own' (*Institutes of Religion*, 20, 'Of Prayer').

More recently, the theologian Karl Barth described prayer as an act of human freedom in response to divine grace—we are free to ask because God has already invited us to do so. Similarly, Simone Weil wrote of prayer as 'attention'—a patient, receptive openness to God that requires letting go of our illusory self-sufficiency (*Gravity and Grace*).

Throughout the Christian tradition runs a common thread: true prayer requires the courage to present ourselves honestly before God, neither inflating our strengths nor hiding our weaknesses, but trusting in God's sovereignty and his gracious response to our genuine need.

Reflection Questions

1. Esther prayed simply, 'Help me', laying bare her fear and vulnerability before God. What makes it difficult for you to be this honest and direct in your own prayers? What might change if you approached God with this level of authenticity?

2. Jesus teaches about persistence in prayer—asking, seeking, knocking. Which of these three actions comes most naturally to you in your relationship with God? Which is most challenging?

3. Both Esther and Bonhoeffer prayed in extreme circumstances facing life-threatening situations. When have you turned to prayer in a time of crisis? How was that prayer different from your everyday prayers?

4. Bonhoeffer's prayer repeatedly contrasts his own condition ('It is dark inside me ... I am lonely ... I am timid ...') with God's character ('with you is the light ... you do not leave me ... with you is my help'). How might this pattern of prayer help you articulate your own needs while affirming your trust in God?

4. Jesus connects prayer (asking of God) with ethical action (doing unto others). How does your experience of receiving from God influence your generosity towards others? Can you identify a specific example of this connection in your life?

Spiritual Practices for the Week

1. The Courage to Ask Prayer: Take a sheet of paper and draw a line down the middle. On the left side, write down areas of your life where you feel vulnerable, afraid, or in need. Be specific and honest. On the right side, write a simple prayer for each need, beginning with 'Help me ...' Use this as a daily prayer guide this week, remembering Esther's directness before God.

2. Lectio Divina with Matthew 7:7-12: Practice this traditional method of praying with Scripture using Jesus' teaching on prayer. Read the passage slowly several times. Choose a word or phrase that stands out to you (perhaps 'ask', 'seek', 'knock', or 'it will be given'). Meditate on this word, pray about what it means for your life, and simply rest in God's presence with this word.

3. Intercessory Courage: Like Esther, practice praying courageously on behalf of others this week. Choose a specific group of people who face injustice or hardship. Find out more about their situation, and then pray specifically for them each day, asking God for both external change and internal courage for those affected.

Closing Prayer

God of all who have had the courage to ask in times of need, we come before you now with open hearts:

Help us, Lord, for we cannot help ourselves. Give us courage to acknowledge our needs, to lay bare our fears and anxieties before you, and to trust in your generous response.

Lord, hear us: *Lord, graciously hear us.*

Where we are in darkness, be our light. Where we are lonely, be our companion. Where we are timid, be our strength. Where we are anxious, be our peace. Where there is bitterness within us, be our patience. Where we do not understand your ways, guide us on the right path.

Lord, hear us: *Lord, graciously hear us.*

Teach us to ask with persistence, to seek with diligence, and to knock with expectation. And as we receive from your abundant goodness, make us generous towards others, that we might do unto them as we would have them do unto us.

Lord, hear us: *Lord, graciously hear us.*

We pray this through Christ, who taught us both to pray with boldness and to love without reserve. *Amen.*

4

Transformation through Trust

Rembrandt Harmenszoon van Rijn (1606-69),
Abraham's Sacrifice,
Etching and Drypoint, 1655.

SCRIPTURE READINGS

After these things the word of the Lord came to Abram in a vision, 'Do not be afraid, Abram, I am your shield; your reward shall be very great'. ² But Abram said, 'O Lord God, what will you give me, for I continue childless, and the heir of my house is Eliezer of Damascus?' ³ And Abram said, 'You have given me no offspring, and so a slave born in my house is to be my heir'. ⁴ But the word of the Lord came to him, 'This man shall not be your heir; no one but your very own issue shall be your heir'. ⁵ He brought him outside and said, 'Look towards heaven and count the stars, if you are able to count them'. Then he said to him, 'So shall your descendants be'. ⁶ And he believed the Lord; and the Lord reckoned it to him as righteousness.

Genesis 15:1-6

¹⁷ Brothers and sisters, join in imitating me, and observe those who live according to the example you have in us. ¹⁸ For many live as enemies of the cross of Christ; I have often told you of them, and now I tell you even with tears. ¹⁹ Their end is destruction; their god is the belly; and their glory is in their shame; their minds are set on earthly things. ²⁰ But our citizenship is in heaven, and it is from there that we are expecting a Saviour, the Lord Jesus Christ. ²¹ He will transform the body of our humiliation that it may be conformed to the body of his glory, by the power that also enables him to make all things subject to himself. 4 ¹ Therefore, my brothers and sisters, whom I love and long for, my joy and crown, stand firm in the Lord in this way, my beloved.

Philippians 3:17-4:1

³⁴ Jesus said to them: 'Jerusalem, Jerusalem, the city that kills the prophets and stones those who are sent to it! How often have I desired to gather your children together as a hen gathers her brood under her wings, and you were not willing! ³⁵ See, your house is left to you. And I tell you, you will not see me until the time comes when you say, "Blessed is the one who comes in the name of the Lord".'

Luke 13:34-35

In the previous three chapters we have been exploring the foundations of 'heart work'—the inward transformation that God seeks to bring about in each of us. From contrasting 'heart work' with 'hard work', to exploring Christ making God's word accessible to our hearts, to considering the courage to ask in prayer—we've been journeying deeper into how God longs to transform us from within.

In this chapter, three Scripture readings invite us to consider yet another dimension of that work: our transformation through trust in God. Each reading gives us an example of how trust in God's good purposes can lead to unexpected change. Each is based on a central premise that is also a promise: when we trust God with our deepest fears and greatest hopes, we open ourselves to a transformation that begins in our hearts and can extend to every aspect of our lives.

Abram's Trust: Looking to the Stars

The first Bible reading we consider in this chapter takes us to a pivotal moment in the life of Abram—a moment so significant that it will lead not only to a changed man but also a changed name: after this encounter God will name him 'Abraham'. God had already called him to leave his homeland, promising to make him the father of a great nation. Now years have passed, and Abram still remained childless. Abram and Sarai have grown old, and so increasingly God's promise seems unlikely to be fulfilled. At this time of uncertainty, the word of the Lord comes to him in a vision: 'Do not be afraid, Abram, I am your shield; your reward shall be very great', God assures him (Genesis 15:1).

Abram's response is strikingly honest. He doesn't hide his doubts: 'O Lord God', he asks, 'what will you give me, for I continue childless, and the heir of my house is Eliezer of Damascus?' (15:2). This is true heart work—Abram laying bare his deepest anxieties before God. Abram doesn't put on a brave face—or even a brave faith—but speaks to God from the heart about what troubles him most. God's promise remains unfulfilled. What is it that God will give him?

God does not respond with rebuke but with reassurance. He takes Abram outside and tells him to open his eyes: 'Look towards heaven and count the stars, if you are able to count them' (15:5). The invitation to 'look towards heaven' is more than a practical instruction. It is an invitation to Abram to let his perspective be changed; his horizon be expanded. Abram is invited to look beyond the immediate limitations of his situation to behold the limitless possibilities of God's promise.

Looking up to heaven is a physical posture that reflects an inward reality. When we fix our eyes on the ground, we only ever see what is directly before us—our current circumstances, our present limitations, our immediate problems. But when we look up, we allow our vision to expand. When we look up, we may see beyond ourselves—and in Abram's case may see something of the vastness of God's creation and the boundlessness of God's power.

This physical posture of looking up can be to us a symbol of the spiritual heart work of trust. Trust requires us to lift our gaze from what seems impossible to what God declares possible. It asks us to shift our focus from the emptiness of our present situation to the fruitfulness of God's promised future.

A Response of Trust

Abram responds to God's invitation to let his vision be changed by a simple—but incredibly important—act of trust: 'Abram believed the

Lord; and the Lord reckoned it to him as righteousness' (15:6). The Hebrew word for 'believed' here, *he'emin*, comes from the same root as our word 'Amen'. It means to consider something as reliable, stable, and firm. Abram doesn't just assent to God's promise; he anchors himself to it. He stakes his life on God's faithfulness. He says Amen to God's promise.

And this trust, this heart work, is 'reckoned to him as righteousness'. Before Abram does anything, before any outward action follows, his trust itself is counted as a right relationship with God. In a world where righteousness was typically measured by work, an outward observance of religious law, this is revolutionary. God does not look at Abram's works and actions, but instead has regard for Abram's heart and faith. God looks at Abram's willingness to trust despite evidence to the contrary—and declares it right work: 'That trust and faith is what I'm looking for. This is what makes our relationship right'. That is heart work—opening our hearts in faith to right living. It requires the adoption of a new attitude; trusting in God not in expectation of any reward for our own work, but coming to trust him entirely as a result of his transforming grace working in us.

What flows from that initial act of heart work is a covenant—a solemn promise, binding God to Abraham and his offspring forever, and vice versa. God, who promised Abraham greatness and a people, pledges himself to Abraham in the same way in which Abraham had pledged himself to trusting God. The gift of entire nations to Abraham's descendants all flows from Abraham's trust in God's vision for him; his Amen to God's purpose for him.

Paul's Invitation: Heavenly Citizenship

The second reading we consider in this chapter, from the epistle to the Philippians, adds another dimension to the transformative work of trusting in God's promises. Paul invites his readers to imitate him as he imitates Christ. Imitation here does not mean superficial mimicry but again it means heart work—adopting the same inner orientation towards God and others that Paul himself has learned from Christ. It means taking on an attitude of humility, self-giving love, and trust in God's purposes even in suffering. Imitating Christ means emptying oneself, making space in our lives for God, so that God can fill us with his grace. Earlier in his letter, Paul described it as having 'the same mind that was in Christ Jesus, who emptied himself and took the form of a servant' (Philippians 2:5-7).

Like Abraham in our first lesson, Paul contrasts this attitude of self-emptying, of opening up space for God in our lives, with the attitude of those whose gaze remains resolutely fixed on the ground—whose 'minds are set on earthly things', as he calls it (3:19). In the same way in which Abraham is being invited to look towards heaven, Paul also invites us to lift our gaze to heaven: 'Our citizenship is in heaven, and it is from there that we are expecting a Saviour, the Lord Jesus Christ' (3:20).

Adopting such a heavenly perspective doesn't mean disengaging from earthly life. Rather, it means seeing our earthly life through God's promises. It means trusting that what we see now is not all there is; that the limitations and sufferings of our present existence have not got the final word. It means letting ourselves not be *conformed* to the ways of the world—'the body of humiliation', as Paul puts it—but instead be *transformed* into the promise of God's glory—'the body of his glory' (see also Romans 12:2).

God's transformative power begins in our hearts and extends even to our bodies. Through our heart work of trust, we open ourselves to a transformation so complete that it encompasses every aspect of our being—heart, soul and body—all can be changed when we engage in this heart work.

Jesus' Trust: The Way to Jerusalem

In the Gospel reading we reflect on in this chapter, we meet Jesus somewhere on his journey from Galilee to Jerusalem. Even though his disciples have not yet grasped this, Jesus knows well that the endpoint of his journey is the cross. When told to get away, because King Herod sought to kill him, Jesus responds not by removing himself from danger, but with clear-eyed determination: 'Listen, I am casting out demons and performing cures today and tomorrow, and on the third day I finish my work', he tells (Luke 13:32).

Jesus knows that his path leads to Jerusalem, the city that 'kills the prophets and stones those who are sent to it' (13:34). Yet he continues resolutely on his way to the cross. In setting his eyes to Jerusalem, Jesus is driven by a love that is so strong it is almost tangible: 'How often have I desired to gather your children together as a hen gathers her brood under her wings,' he laments, 'and you were not willing!' (13:34).

In Jesus, we see human heart work made real at the deepest level: at numerous moments on the long journey to the cross, he is given opportunities to walk away. But at each point, with increasing cost, he makes himself more vulnerable for the sake of love. When faced with rejection and the certainty of suffering and death, he not only continues trusting in God's purposes, but also seeks to gather his own under his wings, shelter them in his protective embrace.

The way in which God fulfils his vision for sinful humanity is costly. Jesus knows that at the end of his earthly life there stands the cross. But by that self-emptying death, God's blessing is brought to a broken world. By Jesus's death on the cross, the narrow horizon of human existence is opened wide, so that when we step outside our own protective walls to stand at the foot of the cross, we may also, like Abraham, come to glimpse the bright canopy of countless stars that reflect to us God's promise.

Trust as Transformation

What does all this mean for us? Like Abraham, you and I are invited to look up—to lift our gaze from our present limitations to the boundless possibilities of God's promises. Like Paul, you and I are called to adopt a heavenly perspective: living as citizens of heaven while navigating the complexities of earthly life. And like Jesus, we are invited to trust God's purposes even when we face resistance or rejection.

This most challenging form of heart work—continuing to trust and remaining open to God when human experience suggests otherwise—is the way of the cross, the way of Christ. Yet with this challenge comes an incredible promise: 'God will transform the body of our humiliation that it may be conformed to the body of his glory' (Philippians 3:21). This transformation begins in our hearts, as we learn to trust God more deeply, love more freely, and hope more confidently.

In my own journey of rehabilitation I've learnt to trust. Every couple of weeks, I would attend the outpatients' clinic at my local hospital for the physiotherapist to check on my progress. As we met, I talked about my frustration that I'd made such little progress in regaining my range of motion. My physiotherapist took precise measurements of my shoulder movement—something I couldn't do for myself. To my surprise, I had actually gained another 15 degrees of motion that I hadn't been able to measure myself.

Something similar happens on our spiritual journey: we often can't accurately measure our own growth. Just as I needed the physiotherapist's objective perspective to recognise my physical healing, so we need other Christians, and a community of faith, to help us recognise the transformation God is working in us, even when—perhaps especially when—we can't see it ourselves.

As we journey on, may we commit ourselves to the heart work of trust: looking up to the stars like Abraham, living as citizens of heaven like Paul, and trusting in God's ultimate triumph, even when, as for Jesus, our path to life transformed and renewed leads through suffering and pain.

Having reflected on how trust opens our hearts to transformation, we'll discover in the next chapter how this inner work inevitably produces an outward movement like a fragrance—the very 'aroma of Christ'—that cannot be contained.

WORKING DEEPER

The concept of trust in Christian Tradition

Throughout Christian history, trust in God has been understood as both a gift and a practice—something we receive by grace yet also cultivate through intentional spiritual disciplines. The early Christian Desert Fathers and Mothers emphasised trust as radical dependence on God rather than self-sufficiency. Abba Antony, the founder of monasticism, taught: 'Our life and our death is with our neighbour. If we win our brother, we win God. If we cause our sister to stumble, we have sinned against Christ' (*Sayings of the Desert Fathers*).

The Cloud of Unknowing, a fourteenth-century mystical text, describes trust as a 'naked intent towards God' that transcends intellectual understanding (*Cloud of Unknowing and The Book of Privy Counselling*). This tradition of apophatic spirituality—seeking to understand God by describing what God is not, rather than what he is—suggests that true transformation comes not from knowing more about God but from trusting more deeply in God's presence, even in darkness and uncertainty.

Half a century or so later than the writer of the *Cloud of Unknowing*, during a time of plague and social upheaval the anchorite Julian of Norwich expressed her theology of deep trust. Her famous words, 'All shall be well, and all shall be well, and all manner of thing shall be well', expressed not optimism but deep trust in God's goodness despite present suffering (*Revelations of Divine Love*). St Julian understood that trust transforms our perception, allowing us to see beyond immediate circumstances to God's larger purposes, to regard our world as secure and as small as a hazelnut in the open hands of Christ.

The Reformers emphasised trust as the essence of faith. Martin Luther described faith as 'a living, daring confidence in God's grace, so sure and certain that someone could stake their life on it a thousand times' (*Preface to the Epistle to the Romans*). For Luther, trust was never a human achievement but God's gift that transformed the believer from within.

Eighty years ago, Dietrich Bonhoeffer wrote from prison about what he called 'this-worldly Christianity'—a trust in God that does not escape from earthly suffering but enters more deeply into it, following Christ's way of the cross.

Reflection Questions

1. Abraham was invited to 'look towards heaven and count the stars'. What might God be inviting you to look up and see beyond your current circumstances? What limitations or impossibilities might God be asking you to see differently?

2. Abraham's response to God was simply to believe—to say 'Amen' to God's promise. In what areas of your life is God inviting you to say 'Amen' despite evidence to the contrary?

3. Paul speaks of our 'citizenship in heaven' while we live on earth. How might this dual citizenship change how you approach your daily responsibilities and challenges?

4. Jesus continued towards Jerusalem despite knowing what awaited him there. When have you needed to trust God's purposes while walking a difficult path? What helped you maintain that trust?

5. Paul writes that God 'will transform the body of our humiliation that it may be conformed to the body of his glory'. What aspects of your life feel most in need of this transforming power? How might trust open you to this transformation?

Spiritual Practices for the Week

1. Stargazing Prayer: On a clear night this week, spend time outside looking at the stars (or look at images of stars such as those on the cover of this book if going outside isn't possible). As you gaze upward, pray Abraham's prayer: 'Lord, I believe you'. Bring to mind specific situations where you need to trust God's promises despite appearances, and repeat this simple prayer.

2. Self-Awareness: Throughout each day, pause briefly before key decisions (what to purchase, how to respond to someone, how to use your time) and ask yourself: 'Am I approaching this as a citizen of heaven or as someone whose mind is set on earthly things?' Notice patterns in your responses.

3. Trust Journey: Create a simple timeline of your life, marking significant moments when you had to trust God despite uncertainty or fear. Reflect on how God was present in those situations, even if you couldn't see it at the time. End by writing a brief prayer of gratitude for God's faithfulness.

Closing Prayer

Faithful God, maker of the stars and keeper of promises, we come before you with our limited vision and our hesitant hearts:

Like Abraham, we sometimes doubt your promises when our circumstances seem to contradict your word. Teach us to look up, beyond our immediate horizons, to see the vastness of your possibilities. Help us to anchor ourselves to your faithfulness, saying 'Amen' to your purposes even when we cannot see the way forward.

Kyrie eleison.

Like Paul, we confess that our minds are often set on earthly things rather than our heavenly citizenship. Transform us by your power, that our humiliation might be conformed to your glory. Reshape our priorities, our desires, and our hopes according to your kingdom rather than this world.

Kyrie eleison.

Like Jesus, give us courage to continue on the path to which you have called us, even when that path leads through difficulty. May we trust so deeply in your purposes that we can gather others under the wings of your love, offering them the same shelter we have found in you.

Kyrie eleison.

We offer this prayer in the name of Jesus Christ, who trusted you perfectly, even unto death, and who lives and reigns with you and the Holy Spirit, one God, forever and ever. *Amen.*

The Aroma of Christ

Andreas Andreani (1558/9-1629)
after Andrea Mantegna (c. 1431-1506),
The Triumph of Julius Caesar,
Chiaroscuro woodcut, 1599.

SCRIPTURE READINGS

[14] But thanks be to God, who in Christ always leads us in triumphal procession, and through us spreads in every place the fragrance that comes from knowing him. [15] For we are the aroma of Christ to God among those who are being saved and among those who are perishing; [16] to the one a fragrance from death to death, to the other a fragrance from life to life. Who is sufficient for these things? [17] For we are not peddlers of God's word like so many; but in Christ we speak as persons of sincerity, as persons sent from God and standing in his presence.

2 Corinthians 2:14-17

Six days before the Passover Jesus came to Bethany, the home of Lazarus, whom he had raised from the dead. [2] There they gave a dinner for him. Martha served, and Lazarus was one of those at the table with him. [3] Mary took a pound of costly perfume made of pure nard, anointed Jesus' feet, and wiped them with her hair. The house was filled with the fragrance of the perfume. [4] But Judas Iscariot, one of his disciples (the one who was about to betray him), said, [5] 'Why was this perfume not sold for three hundred denarii and the money given to the poor?' [6] (He said this not because he cared about the poor, but because he was a thief; he kept the common purse and used to steal what was put into it.) [7] Jesus said, 'Leave her alone. She bought it so that she might keep it for the day of my burial. [8] You always have the poor with you, but you do not always have me'.

John 12:1-8

On our journey together, we have been exploring what we have called 'heart work'—the inward transformation that God seeks to bring about in each of us. From contrasting heart work with hard work, to exploring how Christ makes God's word directly accessible to our hearts, to considering the courage to ask in prayer, to witnessing the transformation of individuals when we trust in God's good purposes for us—our journey has led us deeper into how God changes us from within.

In this chapter, our readings invite us to consider yet another dimension of heart work: how the inward transformation God works in us may be shown forth in our lives. How God's transforming work can radiate outwards to others. And our readings give us a powerful metaphor for this outward movement—that of a beautiful scent or fragrance that emanates. An aroma that fills not just our own lives but the spaces and relationships around us. Genuine heart work produces an aroma—the very aroma of Christ—that cannot be contained.

Mary's Perfume: The Fragrance of Devotion

In the gospel reading we consider in this chapter, we are taken close to Jerusalem, to Bethany, and to a dinner given in Jesus' honour. Just six days before the Passover—less than a week before his crucifixion, Martha serves the meal, Lazarus her brother (whom Jesus had raised from the dead only days earlier) reclines at the table, alive and well. Their sister Mary enters the room, and she carries with her 'a pound of costly perfume made of pure nard' (John 12:3).

What follows is one of the most extravagant acts of devotion recorded in the gospels. Mary takes this perfume—made from resinous trees in the foothills of the Himalayas, imported across the spice route to Jerusalem—and anoints Jesus' feet. Not only does she pour precious perfume worth a year's wages over Jesus' feet. She then proceeds to wipe his feet with her hair. As she pours out her devotion at Jesus' feet, we read that 'the house was filled with the fragrance of the perfume' (12:3).

John's description of the scene really seeks to engage all our senses: as we hear the story, we are not only meant to picture the scene but to smell it. Mary's fragrance isn't contained; it spreads throughout the house. Everyone who is there experiences it. The aroma of Mary's devotion is not something that's just between her and Jesus—but it affects the entire community gathered there. Everybody is able to smell the beautiful perfume that's being poured out over Jesus' feet.

What is true for the perfume in John's story is true for our own heart work. When God transforms us within, the effects of that transformation cannot be contained. If we imagined the transforming work of God as a scent, it would be as if that fragrance could be detected by everyone. It permeates our relationships, our activities, our entire presence in the world—because we emanate something beautiful and costly that has not been there before.

For Mary of Bethany pouring out the costly perfume on Jesus' feet is the culmination of her heart work—her coming to understand who Jesus was and what he meant to her. Earlier in the gospels, we find Mary sitting at Jesus' feet, listening to his teaching while Martha busied herself with tasks (Luke 10:38-42). Now, she returns to those same feet, not just to listen but to pour out her most precious possession. Earlier in John's gospel, we hear her confess her belief that Jesus truly is the resurrection. Now she anoints his body for a grave that she knows will not contain him.

Qualities of Heart Work

Mary's act of devotion shows us a number of qualities that characterise heart work. The first thing to note is that her devotion is costly. The perfume she poured on Jesus' feet was worth three hundred denarii—at the time about a year's wages for a labourer. Mary's gesture was not a calculated, measured response. It's an overflow of devotion that disregarded conventional financial wisdom. Mary spares nothing and gives all.

The second thing to note is how vulnerable Mary makes herself. She literally lets down her hair—something a respectable Jewish woman would not normally do in public. Not only that: she uses her hair as a towel, to wipe Jesus' feet. In doing so, she makes herself vulnerable to criticism, which indeed comes swiftly from Judas.

The last thing to note is that Mary's action is prophetic. When Jesus defends her action, he points out: 'She bought the costly oil so that she might keep it for the day of my burial' (John 12:7). Now it's hard for us to say whether Mary fully understood the implications of her act, or whether she was simply following an intuitive prompting. But I would like to think that her own heart work had so closely aligned her with God's unfolding purposes that she anointed Jesus for burial before anyone else recognised that his burial was imminent.

The fragrance that filled the house that day in Bethany, then, was more than expensive perfume. It was a sacramental action—an outward sign of inward grace. Mary's perfume symbolises the fragrance of wholehearted devotion, the aroma of love poured out without reservation, the grace of a heart so transformed by Jesus that holding anything back was unthinkable.

Becoming the Aroma of Christ

This image of a grace-filled fragrance filling a house finds its parallel in the second reading we consider in this chapter. In his Second Letter to the Corinthians, Paul writes: 'But thanks be to God, who in Christ always leads us in triumphal procession, and through us spreads in every place the fragrance that comes from knowing him'. He continues, by way of an explanation: 'For we are the aroma of Christ to God among those who are being saved and among those who are perishing; to the one a fragrance from death to death, to the other a fragrance from life to life' (2 Corinthians 2:14-16).

In his letter, Paul uses a vivid image from Roman culture—a triumphal procession in which victorious generals would parade their troops through the streets, accompanied by the sweet smell of incense. In Paul's image, Christ is the victorious general and the foot soldiers led in his procession are the people he has claimed for his own—you and I—we are the people led by Christ in triumph. Paul goes even further: we are not merely participants in a procession; we ourselves have become the fragrance that announces Christ's victory.

'We are the aroma of Christ', Paul tells the Corinthians. Not 'we carry the aroma' or 'we distribute the aroma', but 'we *are* the aroma'. We don't just speak about Christ or represent Christ; in some mysterious way, through our heart work we have been transformed to emanate Christ. Our very presence carries the fragrance of his reality. Like Mary's perfume filling the house in Bethany, this aroma of Christ that we become spreads 'in every place'. It cannot be contained or be reserved for certain relationships or settings. Where heart work is real, it permeates all aspects of our lives.

Different Reactions to the Same Aroma

In his letter, Paul introduces a striking paradox. The same aroma leads to opposite reactions in different people. 'To the one a fragrance from death to death, to the other a fragrance from life to life' (2 Corinthians 2:16). The very same Christ-aroma that brings life to some brings a sense of death to others. Looking back on our gospel reading, we can also see this paradox at work. The same perfume that Jesus receives as a beautiful preparation for his burial, Judas condemns as wasteful. The same act that shows forth Mary's devotion triggers Judas's deceit. The fragrance of Christ fills the entire house, but people respond to it differently—some are drawn to it, others recoil.

Genuine heart work—the kind that makes us the aroma of Christ—will inevitably produce mixed reactions. Not everyone welcomes the fragrance of Christ. To some, it is a delightful smell of life and hope. To others, it is a troubling odour of judgement and death to self. Both Mary's act of devotion and Paul's image of being the aroma of Christ point to an important fact: being transformed through Christ, becoming fragrance, is costly. Mary's perfume was worth a year's wages. For that fragrance to fill the house, the jar had to be broken open. The perfume had to be poured out—used up entirely rather than meted out in small portions.

Similarly, for us to become the aroma of Christ requires a similar breaking open—we break open our lives. As Paul says earlier in his letter, 'We have this treasure in clay jars, so that it may be made clear that this extraordinary power belongs to God and does not come from us' (2 Corinthians 4:7). The treasure—the aroma of Christ—is released when the vessel is broken. This is heart work at its most demanding. It requires us to be broken open, to pour ourselves out, to hold nothing back in reserve. It means living with the vulnerability that comes from authentic discipleship, from letting the hearts that have been transformed by God be fully expressed in our words and actions.

Judas's Objection: Calculation vs. Devotion

In the house of Mary, Martha and Lazarus, Judas objected to Mary's extravagance with seemingly practical concerns: 'Why was this perfume not sold for three hundred denarii and the money given to the poor?' (John 12:5). In a seeming aside, John tells us the real motive: 'He said this not because he cared about the poor, but because he was a thief; he kept the common purse and used to steal what was put into it' (12:6). Judas here represents the calculating mind that seeks to limit devotion, to keep it within reasonable bounds, to maintain control. Mary, on the other hand, represents a transformed heart that knows no such bounds, that pours itself out without calculation.

Which are we more like? Do we measure our devotion carefully, making sure it doesn't cost too much or make us too vulnerable? Or are we willing to be broken open, to become the fragrance that fills the house, to be the aroma of Christ?

Jesus defends Mary with striking words: 'Leave her alone. She bought it so that she might keep it for the day of my burial' (John 12:7). He reminds his disciples that Mary's extravagant act of devotion is a preparation for his suffering, death and burial—and, by implication, for his resurrection. The aroma of Christ is always connected to death as well as to life. Paul tells us that to some it is 'a fragrance from death to death, to the other a fragrance from life to life' (2 Corinthians 2:16). The two cannot be separated. The perfume that anoints for burial also fills the house with its living fragrance.

This is the paradox at the heart of our faith: that the way to life leads through death. The path to resurrection passes through the cross. The heart work that transforms us into the aroma of Christ involves both dying and rising with him. As we enter more deeply into our spiritual journey, we are invited to follow Christ on this path—the path of self-giving love that leads to death but doesn't end there. We are called to be broken open like Mary's jar of perfume, to pour ourselves out without reservation, to fill the houses of our lives with the fragrance of Christ.

Beyond Our Own Strength

Letting ourselves be opened up and poured out in this way is not easy. Even Paul, after describing believers as the aroma of Christ, exclaims, 'Who is sufficient for these things?' (2 Corinthians 2:16). On our own, the task of becoming Christ's fragrance in the world is beyond our capacity. If we relied on our own strength or try to manufacture the aroma of Christ through our own efforts that would be hard work. Because true heart work is not our achievement; it is God's gift. The transformation that makes us the aroma of Christ is the work of the Holy Spirit within us. Our part is to yield to this work, to allow ourselves to be broken open, to pour out what God has poured in.

Living as the Aroma of Christ

What does this mean for us as we continue our journey deeper into the open heart of God?

First of all, it invites us to consider the aroma that emanates from our lives. What is it that people experience in our presence? Do they sense something of Christ—his love, his truth, his grace? Or do they smell only our ambition, our anxiety, our judgement? The fragrance we emit reveals the state of our hearts more accurately than our words ever could.

Secondly, it calls us to be willing to be broken open. Mary's perfume could not fill the house until the jar was broken. The aroma of Christ cannot emanate from lives that remain tightly sealed, carefully controlled, invulnerable. Heart work requires that kind of vulnerability—a willingness to let God break open the protective shells we build around ourselves.

Thirdly, it reminds us that the same aroma will produce different reactions. Some will be drawn to the fragrance of Christ in us; others will be repelled by it. We cannot control how others respond to the aroma we emit. Our responsibility is not to manage the reactions of others, but to ensure that what emanates from us is truly the fragrance of Christ, not the odour of our own self-importance or self-righteousness.

And finally, it points us towards the ultimate breaking open and pouring out that occurred on the cross. As we walk the way of the cross with Jesus, we are invited to allow our own lives to be broken open in new ways, to pour ourselves out more completely, to become more fully the aroma of Christ in our world.

In a world filled with the stench of violence, greed, and despair, you and I are called to be a different kind of fragrance—the aroma of Christ: a scent that speaks of love poured out without reservation, of sacrifice that leads to life, of hope that persists even in the face of death.

The aroma of Christ isn't something we manufacture or apply externally. Rather, it emerges naturally from hearts that have been broken open and anointed with his grace. As we receive his healing in our own areas of brokenness, we begin to emanate the distinctive fragrance of a life being restored—a scent that offers hope to others still waiting for their own healing to begin.

During the first weeks after my accident, I would carefully anoint my broken arm with *Pain Away*, an Australian joint and muscle cream. The cream contains arnica, frankincense and essential oils—rosemary, eucalyptus, and lavender. Many of these plants have been used for healing since before the time of Jesus. As I massaged the fragrant cream into my injured shoulder, the smell of these distinctive aromatic oils filled the bathroom. For my family and me the scent—at once astringent and soothing—became linked with healing and relief.

When applied, the cream creates a gentle heat that radiates outwards; much like the scent itself that filled the room—first intense and attention-demanding, then settling into a persistent, warm presence that lingers long after application. In the same way, the fragrance of Christ's presence in our lives may emanate outwards. When we let it permeate, it is detectable by those we encounter. And like my healing balm, which contained frankincense—one of the royal gifts brought to the infant Jesus at his nativity—so our lives can carry the fragrance of devotion and sacrifice, that points to the healing Christ offers to our broken world.

As we journey together, may God give us grace to commit ourselves to the heart work that makes us this fragrance. May we, like Mary, be empowered to break open the most precious parts of ourselves—our hearts—and open them up and pour them out in devotion to Christ. May, through our heart work, the houses of our lives—our homes, our workplaces, our communities—be filled with the unmistakable aroma of Christ.

Having explored how we become the aroma of Christ through our heart work, we'll next turn to how this transformation leads us to bear witness to Christ in word and deed, just as the disciples did on Palm Sunday.

WORKING DEEPER

The Sensory Dimension of Faith

Throughout Christian history, the sensory dimensions of faith—particularly fragrance and aroma—have been recognised as powerful expressions of spiritual reality. In the ancient world, incense was a common feature in both Jewish and pagan worship. The early Christians, initially rejecting incense because of its associations with emperor worship, eventually incorporated it into their liturgies as a symbol of prayer ascending to God and divine presence descending among the people.

The Desert Fathers and Mothers of the fourth century often described holiness as having a perceptible fragrance. Stories abound of saints whose bodies emitted sweet aromas after death—what came to be known as the 'odour of sanctity'. While we might view such accounts sceptically today, they reflect a profound intuition that inner transformation manifests in perceptible ways.

In the medieval period, mystics like St Hildegard of Bingen employed rich sensory language to describe their spiritual experiences. St Hildegard wrote of 'living Light' (*umbra viventis lucis*) that had a 'most pure fountain-like fragrance of strength' (*Scivias*). For her, spiritual realities were not abstract concepts, but experiences that engaged all the senses, including smell.

Eastern Orthodox Christianity has long emphasised the sensory dimension of worship. Writing in the second half of the twentieth century, the Orthodox theologian Alexander Schmemann wrote of the liturgy of the Eucharist as 'the journey of the Church into the dimension of the Kingdom', where heaven and earth are united through sight, sound, touch, taste, and smell (*For the Life of the World*). Incense in Orthodox worship symbolises the presence of the Holy Spirit and the prayers of the faithful rising to God (Revelation 5:8).

The Reformer John Calvin, though often associated with a sober approach to worship, nevertheless wrote eloquently of how believers become 'the aroma of Christ' through their daily lives (*Commentary on Corinthians*). For Calvin, the believers' witness was not primarily about words but about a life so permeated by Christ that it emanated their presence to others.

John Wesley, the founder of Methodism, suggested a 'smell test' for Christian faith. He insisted that true religion must be perceptible in transformed lives and communities. For Wesley, the fragrance of Christ was evident in 'social holiness'—lives of justice, mercy, and love that changed the atmosphere of families, workplaces, and societies (Preface to *Hymns and Sacred Poems*).

More recently, theologians like the Swiss Roman Catholic Hans Urs von Balthasar have explored how all five senses play a role in our perception of God's glory. Von Balthasar argued that beauty—including the 'beautiful fragrance' of Christ—is not merely decorative but revelatory, disclosing God's presence in the world (*The Dramatis Personae: The Person in Christ*).

Reflection Questions

1. Mary's act of devotion was costly and extravagant. What is the most precious thing you possess (whether material or non-material)? What would it mean for you to pour it out in devotion to Christ?

2. Paul writes that we are 'the aroma of Christ'. Think about people you've known whose lives have emanated Christ's presence. What qualities did they exhibit? How did being around them affect you?

3. The same aroma can provoke different reactions in different people. When has your faith or Christian witness evoked unexpected or mixed responses from others? How did you deal with this?

4. Mary's perfume could only fill the house when the jar was broken open. What protective 'jars' in your life might God be asking you to allow to be broken so that Christ's fragrance can spread more freely?

5. Jesus defends Mary's action by connecting it to his coming death and burial. How does the cross—with its themes of sacrifice, surrender, and death to self—inform your understanding of what it means to be 'the aroma of Christ'?

Spiritual Practices for the Week

1. Sensory Prayer: Set aside time each day this week for prayer that engages your sense of smell. Light a candle or incense, or use essential oils, flowers, or other natural fragrances. As you breathe in the aroma, pray that your life might similarly emanate Christ's presence. Pray specifically about relationships or situations where you desire to be more distinctly 'the aroma of Christ'.

2. Breaking Open: Identify something in your life that you've been keeping tightly sealed or controlled—perhaps a gift or talent, a vulnerability, a dream, or a calling. Write this on a slip of paper and place it in a small container. In a prayerful moment, open the container as a symbolic act of offering this area to God, asking that it might become part of how Christ's fragrance emanates from your life.

3. Aroma Awareness: Throughout the week, pay special attention to aromas you encounter—pleasant and unpleasant! Use each encounter as a prompt to ask: 'What spiritual reality might this aroma represent? What in my life or in our world smells like this spiritually?' Let these reflections inform your prayers for transformation—both personal and communal.

Closing Prayer

God of extravagant love, who poured yourself out completely for us in Christ, we come before you with our tightly sealed lives, our carefully measured devotion, our fear of being broken open.

We thank you for Mary's example—her costly perfume poured out without reservation, her vulnerability before others, her prophetic insight that aligned her with your purposes. May we, like her, hold nothing back in our love for you.

Lord, hear us: *Lord, graciously hear us.*

We thank you for Paul's powerful image of being led in your Son's triumphal procession, becoming the very aroma that announces your victory. Forgive us for the times we have emanated not your grace but our own pride, fear, or judgement.

Lord, hear us: *Lord, graciously hear us.*

As we journey together, help us to walk with Jesus on the path that leads through death to life. Break open our lives like Mary's jar of perfume, that the fragrance of Christ might fill the rooms of our existence and draw others into your presence.

Lord, hear us: *Lord, graciously hear us.*

May the houses of our lives—our homes, our workplaces, our communities—be filled with the unmistakable aroma of Christ: the scent of love poured out without reservation, of sacrifice that leads to life, of hope that persists even in the face of death.

Lord, hear us: *Lord, graciously hear us.*

We pray this through Christ our Lord, who lives and reigns with you and the Holy Spirit, one God, forever and ever. *Amen.*

6

The Witnessing Heart

Augustin Hirschvogel (1503-1553),
The Entry into Jerusalem,
Etching, 1547.

SCRIPTURE READINGS

⁶ Shall not everyone taunt the rich and, with mocking riddles, say about them,
⁹ 'Alas for you who get evil gain for your houses,
setting your nest on high
to be safe from the reach of harm!'
¹⁰ You have devised shame for your house
by cutting off many peoples;
you have forfeited your life.
¹¹ The very stones will cry out from the wall,
and the plaster will respond from the woodwork.
¹² 'Alas for you who build a town by bloodshed,
and found a city on iniquity!'
¹³ Is it not from the Lord of hosts
that peoples labour only to feed the flames,
and nations weary themselves for nothing?
¹⁴ But the earth will be filled
with the knowledge of the glory of the Lord,
as the waters cover the sea.

Habakkuk 2:6, 9-14

²⁹ When Jesus had come near Bethphage and Bethany, at the place called the Mount of Olives, he sent two of the disciples, ³⁰ saying, 'Go into the village ahead of you and, as you enter it, you will find tied there a colt that has never been ridden. Untie it and bring it here. ³¹ If anyone asks you, "Why are you untying it?" just say this, "The Lord needs it".' ³² So those who were sent departed and found it as he had told them. ³³ As they were untying the colt, its owners asked them, 'Why are you untying the colt?' ³⁴ They said, 'The Lord needs it'. ³⁵ Then they brought it to Jesus; and after throwing their cloaks on the colt, they set Jesus on it. ³⁶ As he rode along, people kept spreading

their cloaks on the road. ³⁷ As he was now approaching the path down from the Mount of Olives, the whole multitude of the disciples began to praise God joyfully with a loud voice for all the deeds of power that they had seen, ³⁸ saying,

'Blessed is the king
who comes in the name of the Lord!
Peace in heaven,
and glory in the highest heaven!'

³⁹ Some of the Pharisees in the crowd said to him, 'Teacher, order your disciples to stop'. ⁴⁰ He answered, 'I tell you, if these were silent, the stones would shout out'.

Luke 19:29-40

We are almost at the culmination of our journey through Lent. In the previous chapters we have been contrasting heart work with hard work, then explored the themes of trust and transformation, the courage to ask and, in the previous chapter, becoming the aroma of Christ.

As we consider Jesus' triumphal entry into Jerusalem, we meet another dimension of heart work: the witnessing heart. In Luke's account of Jesus riding into the Holy City, we encounter people who have been so transformed by Jesus' presence that they bear courageous public testimony to who he is and what he has done. The disciples who have journeyed with Jesus become bold prophetic voices proclaiming his kingship. Their hearts, having been opened by Christ, now work to open the hearts of others to receive Christ, by making his deeds of transformation known to the world.

The Triumphal Entry: Hearts Overflowing with Testimony

Luke's Gospel of the Palms takes us to Jerusalem, where Jesus will face the harshest rejection by the authorities—arrest, a slanderous trial, and a cruel death. But before that final rejection, there is a moment of recognition and acclaim. Jesus has particular and peculiar instructions to his disciples to prepare for his entry into Jerusalem: 'Go into the village ahead of you, and as you enter it you will find tied there a colt that has never been ridden. Untie it and bring it here' (Luke 19:30).

The disciples follow Jesus' instructions without fully understanding their purpose, John tells us in his gospel (John 12:16). Only after the resurrection did they understand that Zechariah's prophecy that Zion's king would enter Jerusalem 'humble and riding on a donkey, on a colt, the foal of a donkey', was being fulfilled in their presence (Zechariah 9:9, John 12:16b). They bring the colt, drape it with their garments, and 'set Jesus on it' (19:35).

As he processes into the city, people spread their cloaks on the dusty road, creating a carpet of garments. All those whom he had called away from their previous occupations and responsibilities, whose hearts he had opened, and who had become his followers, acclaim him as their ruler: 'Blessed is the king who comes in the name of the Lord! Peace in heaven, and glory in the highest heaven!', they shout (19:38). They had witnessed his works of power—had seen him heal, drive out demons, had even seen him raise people from the dead. They had heard him teach about God's kingdom. They had experienced his love and grace first-hand. Now, they cannot remain silent. Their mouths speak from the abundance of their hearts. They become joyful witnesses to his word and works.

And the authorities demand their silence: 'Teacher, order your disciples to stop', they command (Luke 19:39). But Jesus replies, 'I tell you, if these were silent, the stones would shout out' (19:40). The very stones of Jerusalem would testify to Christ's call to turn from the ways of this world to the way of heaven. Christ here cites the very prophets that have been sent by God to correct and chastise his people, many of whom found Jerusalem to be the city that kills the prophets and those that are sent to it.

The Stones Cry Out: Habakkuk's Warning

We read the prophecy that Jesus cites here in the first Scripture reading we consider for this chapter. Six centuries before the advent of Christ, the prophet Habakkuk carried God's chastisement to those who oppress others and seek only after their own gain. He rebuked them in God's name: those who take away the possessions of others would lose their own. Those who shed the blood of others, would themselves die by the sword. The very stones of their homes would accuse them; the plaster and the wooden beams would call out their wickedness. God's knowledge and glory would cover the earth in spite of the evil actions of the rich and powerful. When God's people are silenced, the very stones that make up the homes of the oppressors call out their bloodshed and iniquity, we read (Habakkuk 2:9-14). They will witness to God regardless.

The Call to Witness: Heart Work Made Visible

Bearing witness to the words, works and judgement of God is another important aspect of heart work. Followers of Jesus are called to witness to the One who gave his own life so that all might have life in abundance. Disciples are called to witness to the One who won redemption for us on the cross by our advocating and working for those who stand in need of release of the structures of injustice that hold them enthralled. As followers of Jesus, we are entrusted with the ministry of showing forth his presence in our world; and we show forth that presence in our treatment and work for others. We become witnesses to the One who gave his life on the cross, by helping to shoulder the burdens of our fellows, by speaking out against the injustices faced by our fellows, and by advocating and fighting on their behalf.

That might sound a bit political. The reason why Jesus was on the one hand greeted triumphantly by his followers and rejected by the authorities is that his good news is political. Jesus' teaching addresses society as a whole; speaks to the whole *pólis* (the ancient Greek city state, from which we derive our word 'political'). Jesus' teaching challenges our contemporary world order by its uncompromising message of a world turned upside down by the values of the kingdom of God. The gospels proclaim a future in which the rich are brought low, and the lowly lifted up; where strangers are deliberately included—'those who have been far off brought near'—and where the first may end up the last.

The good news of Jesus is political, but the politics of the kingdom of heaven are not aligned with any political party. The politics of the kingdom are aligned with the values of the gospel that Jesus preached: showing forth the compassion of Christ, who emptied himself so that all might be filled with grace. And this message is vital to share in a world that hurts so much, and is longing for the message of compassion, peace and grace. Sharing that message needs witnesses.

Stones that Speak: The Witness of Buildings and Communities

Throughout history, even buildings have been pressed into service as witnesses to the gospel message. For over a decade—from 2013-23—St Paul's Cathedral in Melbourne, which I lead, had a ten-metre-high banner on its South Spire that read: 'Let's fully welcome refugees'. Our building shared in our proclamation, with the stones of the spire sharing the message that we taught and told: that refugees are welcomed here, that we seek to support and empower refugees, and that we will stand up for people facing injustice and cruelty.

During the decade in which the banner was displayed, before it had frayed so much that it needed to be taken down in case it would rip off in a storm, the witness of the stones combined with the witness of our community, transformed our Cathedral. Refugees saw the sign and asked what the church did to welcome displaced people. And we told them about our free English Classes, information sessions about working rights in Australia, and our support in making applications for asylum. Our community grew to be more international, and learnt as much from the refugees in their midst as they learnt from the community. A dozen years on, our congregation includes members from across the globe—displaced people as well as migrants, people for whom their Christian faith was the reason they had to flee their homeland, as well as people who came to faith because of the welcome they received.

This is just one example of how stones—physical structures and institutions—can join with human voices in bearing witness to the gospel. All over the world, church buildings stand as built witnesses to the values of God's kingdom, whether through their architecture designed to draw the eye heavenwards, their placement at the heart of communities, the gospel messages displayed in their windows, their inscriptions or wall-decorations. When human witnesses falter, the stones themselves continue to cry out.

The Dimensions of Witnessing

You and I are called to be witnesses to God's transforming love. That is another important aspect of our heart work. As Jesus enters the Holy City, I invite you to reflect on three dimensions of what it means to open our hearts and bear witness to Christ's transforming love:

First of all, let's think about how our own hearts can help us bear witness to Christ. In the gospel reading we considered, the disciples could not remain silent about what they had seen and experienced. Their hearts overflowed with testimony because they had been transformed by Christ's presence. What things has Christ done in your life that deserve to be shared? Perhaps it was a moment of healing, a time when you felt deeply loved despite your failures, or a gradual transformation that others have noticed in you. The most authentic witness to Christ's transforming love does not come because we feel obligation to speak of his grace, but because our hearts have been genuinely touched by grace.

Secondly, how might our witness take concrete form in action? Our Cathedral's 'Let's fully welcome refugees' banner was powerful because it was not empty words—it was backed by ministries of welcome: free English classes and practical support, and a loving community. Our witness also should never be empty words, but has to combine proclamation and practice. Witnessing hearts should be matched by hands that serve, feet that stand alongside others, and voices that speak out for those who cannot speak for themselves.

Thirdly, what risks might your witness entail? The authorities demanded the disciples' silence because their proclamation threatened the status quo. True witness—whether to Christ's sovereignty over our lives or to the injustices of our day—will invariably encounter resistance. Yet Jesus assures us that even if human voices are silenced, the very stones will cry out. The question is not whether the truth will be proclaimed, but whether you and I have the courage and strength to be the messengers of the kingdom of God.

A Vision of Transformation

As we move from Palm Sunday deeper into Holy Week, our witnessing hearts will be tested as we follow Christ to the cross. And so, as we prepare to walk with Jesus through his passion, death, and resurrection, I invite you to open your hearts wide to God and witness his love for you, so that you may be equipped to speak of that love to those around you. The inward transformation God has been working in us is meant to overflow into our families, our workplaces, our community, and our world. Like the stones of the Cathedral I serve, which proclaimed a welcome when human voices were dismissed, our lives are meant to testify to Christ's love even when words fail us.

The peace and glory of heaven that the disciples proclaimed at the gates of Jerusalem is never meant to remain confined to heaven. Their song envisioned a world transformed by the values of God's kingdom—where the last are first, where strangers are welcomed, where the knowledge of the glory of the Lord will cover the earth, as the waters cover the sea (Habakkuk 2:14). When Christians bear witness to those values in word and deed, when you and I speak and work for God's kingdom to be shown forth in the places where God has put us, we take our share in making God's vision for our world more real. May we, like those first disciples on the road to Jerusalem, find the courage to keep proclaiming 'Blessed is the king who comes in the name of the Lord!' even when others would prefer that we remained silent. And may our hearts, transformed by God's grace, become more compassionate for the suffering of others.

The eve of Palm Sunday marked a significant milestone in my recovery—having slowly returned to riding my bike again, I completed a 50-kilometer ride through the Yarra Valley. As disciples witnessing to Christ, we often carry forward the very areas of our lives that once experienced wounding. Paradoxically, our greatest witness frequently emerges from our deepest vulnerabilities. My return to cycling the kind of distances I used to ride with ease before my accident, was a reminder of trusting in the healing process even when progress seemed slow and imperceptible. In ministry I have found that our own witness often shines brightest through the areas where God has most profoundly restored us. Because hearts that have been broken open to compassion more readily open to others experiencing similar brokenness. When we share our brokenness—in ways that are pastorally appropriate and helpful—we engage in witnessing to the grace of healing.

As Palm Sunday gives way to Holy Week, our journey leads us finally to the cross—where we witness not our own heart work, but God's ultimate heart work revealed in Christ's self-offering for us and all humanity on the cross.

WORKING DEEPER

Christian Witness Through the Ages

The call to bear witness has been central to Christian identity from the beginning. The Greek word for 'witness', *mártys*, is the root of our English word 'martyr'. In the early church, witness often meant being willing to suffer or die rather than deny Christ. St Polycarp, St Perpetua, St Felicity and their companions, among countless others showed how witnessing to our faith might cost everything.

But witness has always been more than verbal testimony. The second-century *Epistle to Diognetus* by an anonymous 'student of the apostles' (*apostólōn genoménos mathetēs*) described Christians as those who 'pass their time upon the earth, but are citizens of heaven. They obey the prescribed laws, and at the same time surpass the laws by their lives'. Their distinctive way of life—loving enemies, caring for the outcast, refusing to participate in emperor worship—spoke as loudly as their words.

The Reformers emphasised that our witness must be grounded in Scripture. For them, authentic testimony to Christ meant proclaiming the gospel as revealed in God's word, not human tradition. This led to efforts to translate the Bible into vernacular languages so that all believers could bear witness from a place of personal engagement with the text.

In his *Cost of Discipleship* Dietrich Bonhoeffer wrote of 'costly discipleship' that refuses 'cheap grace'—a witness that challenges both secular and religious complacency. Similarly, Martin Luther King Jr.'s witness against racial injustice was rooted in his understanding of the gospel's demands. 'The church must be reminded', King wrote, 'that it is not the master or the servant of the state, but rather the conscience of the state' (*A Knock at Midnight*).

The Orthodox theologian Alexander Schmemann described the church's witness as 'the sacrament of the Kingdom'—making present in the world the reality of God's reign (*The Eucharist: Sacrament of the*

Kingdom). For Schmemann, everything from liturgy to social action was meant to reveal the transformative power of God's kingdom.

Through all these expressions of Christian witness runs a common thread: authentic testimony to Christ involves both proclamation and embodiment, both speaking truth and living it out in community. Christian witness is never merely individual but always communal, never merely verbal but always incarnational—rooted in life and community.

Reflection Questions

1. The disciples could not remain silent about what they had seen and experienced with Jesus. What aspects of your experience with Christ feel most compelling to share with others? What holds you back from doing so?

2. Jesus said that if his disciples were silent, 'the stones would shout out'. In what ways might the physical spaces you inhabit (your home, workplace, church building) bear witness to God's kingdom? How might you make these spaces a more explicit testimony to the values of Christ?

3. The banner on St Paul's Cathedral Melbourne proclaimed welcome to refugees, backed by practical ministries of welcome. What issue of justice or compassion particularly stirs your heart? How might you bear witness to Christ's values in relation to this issue, through both words and actions?

4. The authorities demanded silence from Jesus' followers because their testimony threatened the status quo. When have you experienced push-back or resistance because of your Christian witness? How did you respond?

5. The disciples proclaimed Jesus as king at a time when such language was politically dangerous. In what ways might faithful Christian witness still challenge political powers and structures today? How do you navigate the political implications of the gospel in your own context?

Spiritual Practices for the Week

1. Journalling Witness: Set aside time each day this week to write about moments when you have experienced Christ's presence, grace, or transformative power in your life. Consider which of these experiences may be appropriate to share with others. You may want to choose one story to share with a trusted friend or family member as a practice of verbal witness.

2. Visual Witness: Create a small visual representation of your beliefs or faith-values that could become a conversation starter. This might be a symbol displayed in your home or workspace, artwork you create, or even a thoughtful social media post. Notice what opportunities for witness arise from this visual prompt.

3. Justice Witness: Choose an issue of justice that resonates with your understanding of the gospel. Research one concrete action you can take this week to bear witness to Christ's values in relation to this issue. This might be contacting an elected official, supporting an organisation financially, volunteering, or participating in a public action. Reflect on how this connects to your faith in Christ.

Closing Prayer

God of prophets and disciples, who calls us to bear witness to your transforming love, we thank you for the courage of those who first proclaimed Jesus as king. Their hearts, transformed by his presence, could not remain silent about what they had seen and heard:

We confess that we are often timid in our witness, hesitant to speak of your grace or stand for your justice. We fear rejection, misunderstanding, or isolation. Forgive our silence when we should have spoken, our inaction when we should have stood up, our comfort when we should have risked.

Lord, in your mercy: *hear our prayer.*

As we enter Holy Week, open our eyes anew to the wonder of Christ's love, shown in his willing journey to the cross. May our hearts be so transformed by this love that we cannot help but testify to it— in word and deed, in public and private, in comfort and in cost.

Lord, in your mercy: *hear our prayer.*

Make us brave witnesses to your upside-down kingdom, where the last are first, the humble are exalted, and enemies are embraced as friends. And when our voices falter or are silenced, remind us that even the stones will cry out, for your truth cannot be contained.

Lord, in your mercy: *hear our prayer.*

We make our prayer in the name of Jesus Christ, the king who comes in the name of the Lord, and now lives and reigns with you and the Holy Spirit, one God, now and forever. *Amen.*

7

The Open Heart of God

Annibale Carracci (1560-1609),
Pietà (The Christ of Caprarola),
Etching, Engraving and Drypoint.

SCRIPTURE READINGS

[18] For the message about the cross is foolishness to those who are perishing, but to us who are being saved it is the power of God. [19] For it is written,

> 'I will destroy the wisdom of the wise,
> and the discernment of the discerning I will thwart'.

[20] Where is the one who is wise? Where is the scribe? Where is the debater of this age? Has not God made foolish the wisdom of the world? [21] For since, in the wisdom of God, the world did not know God through wisdom, God decided, through the foolishness of our proclamation, to save those who believe. [22] For Jews demand signs and Greeks desire wisdom, [23] but we proclaim Christ crucified, a stumbling block to Jews and foolishness to Gentiles, [24] but to those who are the called, both Jews and Greeks, Christ the power of God and the wisdom of God. [25] For God's foolishness is wiser than human wisdom, and God's weakness is stronger than human strength.

1 Corinthians 1:18-25

So they took Jesus; [17] and carrying the cross by himself, he went out to what is called The Place of the Skull, which in Hebrew is called Golgotha. [18] There they crucified him, and with him two others, one on either side, with Jesus between them. [19] Pilate also had an inscription written and put on the cross. It read, 'Jesus of Nazareth, the King of the Jews'. [20] Many of the Jews read this inscription, because the place where Jesus was crucified was near the city; and it was written in Hebrew, in Latin, and in Greek. [21] Then the chief priests of the Jews said to Pilate, 'Do not write, "The King of the Jews", but, "This man said, I am King of the Jews".' [22] Pilate answered, 'What I have written I have written'. [23] When the soldiers had crucified Jesus, they took his clothes and divided them into four parts, one for each soldier. They also took his tunic; now the tunic was seamless, woven in one piece from the top. ²⁴ So they said to one another, 'Let us not tear it, but cast lots for it to see who will get it'. This was to fulfill what the Scripture says,

'They divided my clothes among themselves,
and for my clothing they cast lots'.

²⁵ And that is what the soldiers did.

Meanwhile, standing near the cross of Jesus were his mother, and his mother's sister, Mary the wife of Clopas, and Mary Magdalene. ²⁶ When Jesus saw his mother and the disciple whom he loved standing beside her, he said to his mother, 'Woman, here is your son'. ²⁷ Then he said to the disciple, 'Here is your mother'. And from that hour the disciple took her into his own home.

²⁸ After this, when Jesus knew that all was now finished, he said (in order to fulfill the Scripture), 'I am thirsty'. ²⁹ A jar full of sour wine was standing there. So they put a sponge full of the wine on a branch of hyssop and held it to his mouth. ³⁰ When Jesus had received the wine, he said, 'It is finished'. Then he bowed his head and gave up his spirit.

John 19:16-30

In the previous chapters we have been exploring what we have called 'heart work'—the inward transformation that God seeks to bring about in each of us. We began in our first chapter by contrasting heart work with hard work, noting how God calls us not to outward religious observance but to inward renewal. We have explored the themes of trust and transformation, looked at the courage it takes to ask God for help, considered what it means to become the aroma of Christ as the signs of our inner transformation emanate outwards, and reflected on our call to bear witness to Christ in word and deed.

In this chapter, which you may wish to read on Good Friday, we come to the culmination of our reflections—and indeed, to the culmination of all heart work: the cross of Christ. Because at the cross, we witness the ultimate heart work—not our own, but God's. In what appears to the world as defeat and humiliation, people of faith may recognise the wisdom and the power, the healing and the consolation that God seeks to give his world. As Paul writes in the first reading we consider for this chapter, 'The message about the cross is foolishness to those who are perishing, but to us who are being saved it is the power of God' (1 Corinthians 1:18).

As we look on the broken body of Jesus this Good Friday, we behold the open heart of God—the depths of divine love revealed. We bring our own brokenness—and the hearts that God has broken open through our Lenten heart work—to the foot of the cross. Yet our coming to the foot of the cross is more than passive witnessing or contemplation. It is an invitation to engage in a final, culminating aspect of heart work: to place the cross within our own hearts, making the depths of our being a sanctuary in which the crucified and risen Lord may dwell.

Placing the Cross into our Hearts

In Johann Sebastian Bach's monumental *St John Passion*, the German composer placed a beautiful chorale after the account of Christ's crucifixion. The hymn Bach chose was written in 1613, during a plague outbreak in Silesia, by the Lutheran pastor Valerius Herberger. As he buried more than two thousand members of his congregation, Herberger expressed his grief and faith in poetry. He imagined the human heart as a sanctuary where Christ's cross stands tall—not as an instrument of torture, but as a source of consolation. A bright jewel, that 'sparkles for all time and at all hours'; giving courage and hope even in times of suffering and death. As Jesus hangs on the cross, with Pilate's inscription 'Jesus of Nazareth, the King of the Jews' placed above his head, the choir sings these moving words on behalf of the congregation:

In meines Herzens Grunde
Dein Nam' und Kreuz allein
Funkelt zu aller Stunde
Drauf kann ich fröhlich sein.
Erschein mir in dem Bilde
Zu Trost in meiner Not
Wie du, Herr Christ, so milde
Dich hast geblut' zu Tod.

In the depths of my heart,
Your name and cross alone
Sparkles for all time and at all hours,
Because of it I can be cheerful.
Appear to me in the picture
For consolation in my adversity
As you, Lord Christ, so charitable
You have bled to death!

How might we create a sanctuary in the depths of our heart—at the core of being—for Christ, and what might it mean for us to open our hearts to receive the 'name and cross' of Jesus, as a shining beacon that lights up our heart 'for consolation in [our] adversity'? Consecrating our hearts as a sanctuary for Christ means undertaking the heart work that we thought about in this book. As we reflect about our hearts becoming a sanctuary for Christ, three aspects of that heart work in particular stand out.

First of all, opening ourselves to the cross means making ourselves vulnerable: it means letting ourselves be broken open to compassion. In the same way in which Jesus was broken on the cross, so we open ourselves to pain and suffering. We cannot receive the cross of Christ in hearts that remain tightly sealed, carefully guarded against pain or intrusion, we learnt in chapter 5. Hearts that receive the cross must be willing to be real. Rather than hearts of stone, ours need to be hearts of flesh—ready to feel pain in the same way in which Christ feels ours—in order to make a home for the cross (see Ezekiel 36:26).

Secondly, it means setting apart a sacred space within ourselves. Jesus' contemporaries believed that the Temple in Jerusalem contained the holy of holies where God's presence dwelt on earth. But Christ's death breaks down the barriers that confined God's presence to one place. When he died on the cross, the Temple veil was rent in two, opening God's sanctuary to the world. Through the cross, God's heart is opened wide, inviting all people to receive his divine presence. And when we open our hearts to God, we declare that at our very core—that private space known fully only to us—there is holy ground. That, surely, is what Paul meant when he prayed that 'Christ may dwell in your hearts through faith' (Ephesians 3:17)—that we set aside our hearts as a dwelling place for the crucified God.

Finally, receiving the cross into our hearts means receiving a permanent imprint in our being. Many of us wear a cross round our necks to say that we belong to Jesus. Having Christ's cross placed in our hearts is not like the crosses we can put on and take off again. Receiving Christ's cross in our hearts marks us permanently as Christ's own. Receiving his cross means reorienting our hopes, desires, even our relationships—so that they are redefined through the cross. Our lives are made more Christ-shaped when we open ourselves to receive the image and imprint of his cross in our hearts.

Glory in Suffering

In the story of the Passion told by St John, something remarkable happens: suffering and glory become inseparably intertwined. Christ is glorified by his deepest humiliation, the evangelist knows from the outset of his story (John 1:11). The fulfilment, the highpoint, of his ministry is his being lifted high on a cross, for all to see (John 12:28, 33). Rather than a tragic moment of despair, the cross is the moment of ultimate triumph and fulfilment. This is the great paradox of our faith: that the crucifixion is at once Jesus's deepest humiliation and his greatest glorification.

In the chorale in Bach's *St John Passion*, the cross that shines brightly like a jewel in the hearts of believers is the same cross on which Jesus suffered and died. The instrument of torture becomes a beacon of hope that reflects divine light. The first reading we consider for this chapter, from 1 Corinthians, reflects on this paradox. There Paul describes the cross as 'a stumbling block to Jews and foolishness to Gentiles, but to those who are the called, both Jews and Greeks, Christ the power of God and the wisdom of God' (1 Corinthians 1:23-24). Paul knows that the cross is wisdom and power, because it reveals God's plan for this world: the obedient Son of Man who, in letting himself be lifted up high on a cross, will draw all people to himself (John 12:32).

When Jesus spoke these words of premonition, just days before his own crucifixion, he added, 'while you have the light, believe in the light, so that you may become children of light' (John 12:36). Jesus knew that he would be lifted high on a cross. He knew that the Father's will for him would be fulfilled in his giving his life so that all might have life forever. As he died at midday, the sun hid its face. Yet the light of life shone on: even as the sun went dark, the Son of God shone forth, so that everyone who believes in him should not remain in darkness (John 12:46). That shining light of the cross is offered to us as a sign of consolation, a light to walk by, when we open our hearts to receive it.

Sharing in Christ's Passion

Where people open their hearts to receive the cross of Christ in their lives, they participate in the Passion of Christ. Our pain becomes united with his pain; our brokenness with his brokenness. I do not want to suggest that pain is good in itself. Rather, when we open our hearts to receive the sign of the cross, we open our hearts to God's very presence in us. In the midst of grief, loss, or despair, the cross in our hearts 'sparkles for all time and at all hours'. The cross illumines us from within, shining light into our darkness, assuring us that suffering will not have the final word.

When the cross stands in our hearts, our own sufferings may be transformed. Our suffering is not erased or denied—remember how following his resurrection Christ showed his wounds to his disciples to show that he had truly risen from the dead (John 20:27)? The wounds remain. But our suffering is reoriented, given a new fixed point. Literally so: as Jesus dies he exclaims, 'It is finished' (John 19:30). The Greek word used here, *tetélestai*, comes from the word *teléō*—to bring to a goal, to bring to an endpoint. On the cross, Jesus brings to completion, to fulfilment, to perfection, the work of God. As he dies, he announces the completion of God's work of love. The open heart of God accomplishes what nothing else could—the reconciliation of humanity with God, the defeat of sin and death, and the renewal of all creation.

People who have Christ's cross enthroned in their hearts are enabled to share in the work of renewal and reconciliation. People whose hearts are open to the suffering God are drawn into what we might call 'com-passion'—literally, 'suffering with'. The heart of God, opened wide on the cross, enables our own hearts to break open in love for the world. This is not mere empathy, though it includes that. It is deeper—a mutual indwelling where Christ suffers in us and we in him. As Paul told the Galatians: 'I have been crucified with Christ; and it is no longer I who live, but it is Christ who lives in me' (Galatians 2:19-20).

When we place the cross into our hearts, we can become channels of Christ's own compassion for the world. And when we begin to see others through the eyes of the Crucified One, our own presence in places of suffering can become redemptive. Because we carry his cross in our own hearts, we carry Christ's compassion to our broken world.

And it is through those acts of compassion that others may encounter the crucified and risen Lord: because we witness to the suffering of others.

Jesus Breathes out his Spirit

Our heart work of enthroning Christ's cross is never merely private or personal. It always leads us outwards in love and service. As Jesus breathed his last on the cross, John tells us that he 'bowed his head and gave up his spirit' (John 19:30). The Greek word for spirit, *pneūma*, is the same word also used for breath. The final breath of Jesus becomes, in a sense, the first breath of the church—the people who, redeemed through the cross, and empowered by the sending of the Holy Spirit, continue Christ's presence and work in the world so that all might know the One who grants life in abundance.

When we enthrone the cross in our hearts, we are empowered by this same Holy Spirit to do Christ's work in the world. We become part of the ongoing story of God's love, extending the compassion of the cross to all who suffer, and place their cares and burdens into the care of Christ.

The Cross in Today's World

What does this mean for us today, as we witness suffering and injustice in our world? How does the heart work of placing Christ's cross in our innermost selves shape our response to the challenges and sufferings of our time? Three particular pressing situations spring to mind:

As we look at conflicts around the world, especially when the lands of Christ's crucifixion and many other places are soaked with blood, the cross in our hearts calls us to stand with all who suffer. People of the cross are people of compassion. And that means shunning simplistic narratives that demonise one side while absolving the other. But rather means weeping with grieving people on all sides of the conflict.

People of the cross are those who persist in seeking paths to peace when political or military solutions seem impossible.

As we confront climate change, the cross in our hearts is a painful reminder that creation itself 'groans in labour pains, awaiting redemption' (Romans 8:22). Those who have Christ's cross in their hearts are called to act decisively—fasting from fossil fuels and standing in solidarity with the most vulnerable: our neighbouring island nations facing rising seas, our farming communities battling extreme weather, and the species that are on the brink of extinction. The cross challenges us towards simpler lives that prioritise the common good over our own convenience, well-being or profit.

And, finally, as we witness injustice in our own nations and cities—the growing divide between rich and poor, the ongoing disadvantage faced by First Nations peoples, the hostile treatment of asylum seekers, the isolation of the elderly, and the loneliness of the young—the cross in our hearts compels us to action. Not out of a sense of guilt or political ideology, but because of the compassionate presence of Christ—the shining cross of Christ—within us.

The Open Heart of God

On Good Friday, we stand before the open heart of God—broken open in love for us and for all creation. We see in the cross not defeat but victory, not the end of hope but its deepest fulfilment. As we stand at the foot of the cross, you and I are invited to let our own hearts be broken open in surrender to the One who loves us beyond measure. We are called to enthrone the cross in the depths of our being, so that it 'sparkles for all time and at all hours', as a source of consolation in our own times of adversity. And we are invited to let its light and life flow through us, as a wellspring of strength, for our sharing the compassion of Christ in a world still yearning for healing, justice, and peace.

As I write this chapter, my arm is much improved but not yet fully restored to its pre-accident condition. The work of healing continues. This ongoing nature of healing is a good reminder to me of the reality of heart work in our spiritual lives. Yes, the cross means that Christ's work is completed—'It is finished'—but our participation in that completed work unfolds gradually throughout our lives. My physiotherapist reminded me that healing is not linear; it involves progress and plateaux, breakthroughs and setbacks. Similarly, our heart work with God follows a rhythm of growth that respects our human limitations while steadily directing us towards wholeness. In this ongoing journey, both physical and spiritual, we learn to trust that the God who calls us close to his open heart will be faithful in working in and through us.

WORKING DEEPER

The Heart of God in Christian Tradition

Throughout Christian history, the image of God's heart opened in love for humanity has found profound expression. The early Church Fathers often spoke of Christ's side, pierced by the soldier's spear, as the source from which the church was born. Just as in Genesis Eve was formed from Adam's side, the Church Fathers saw the church emerging from the wound in Christ's side, with the water and blood symbolising the sacraments of Baptism and the Eucharist.

St Augustine wrote of God's heart as the divine interior life into which believers are invited through grace: 'Late have I loved you, O Beauty ever ancient, ever new, late have I loved you! You were within me, but I was outside, and it was there that I searched for you' (*Confessions*). For St Augustine, the cross creates access to God's inner life—the heart of God previously hidden is now revealed and made accessible.

Medieval spirituality developed a rich devotion to the open heart of Jesus, most notably in the writings of women mystics like St

Gertrude the Great of Helfta and St Mechthild of Hackeborn. St Gertrude described a vision in which she rested her head on Christ's wounded side and heard the beating of his heart (*A Herald of Divine Love*). This intimacy with the suffering Christ became central to medieval piety—not as a morbid fascination with pain but as profound identification with divine love shown forth in vulnerability.

St Julian of Norwich offers perhaps the most remarkable meditation on Christ's open heart: 'And with this our good Lord said most blessedly, "Behold how I love you", as if he had said, "My darling, behold and see your Lord, your God, who is your maker and your endless joy. See your own brother, your Saviour".' (*Revelations of Divine Love*). Dame Julian understands the cross as the revelation of God's unconditional love—a love that has always existed but is most fully shown forth in Christ's passion.

More recently, theologians like Hans Urs von Balthasar have explored how the cross reveals the inner life of the Trinity (*Mysterium Paschale*). For von Balthasar, Christ's abandonment on the cross discloses a 'distance' within God that can embrace all human alienation. The cry 'My God, my God, why have you forsaken me?' (Psalm 22:1, Mark 15:34, Matthew 27:46) reveals not the absence of God but the presence of divine love that can reach into the furthest extremes of human suffering.

Liberation theologians like Gustavo Gutiérrez have emphasised that God's open heart on the cross represents God's preferential option for the poor and suffering (*A Theology of Liberation*). The crucified God identifies particularly with history's victims, standing in solidarity with all who are oppressed and marginalised.

Across the Christian tradition runs a common understanding: that in Christ crucified, we encounter not just a demonstration of divine love but an invitation into God's very heart—to dwell there and to allow that same heart to dwell in us.

Reflection Questions

1. The hymn in Bach's *St John Passion* describes the cross as 'in the depths of my heart, your name and cross alone sparkles for all time and at all hours'. What might it mean for the cross to become a source of light within you, especially in times of darkness or suffering?

2. Receiving the cross into our hearts means making ourselves vulnerable. What protective barriers have you built around your heart that might need to be removed to make room for Christ's cross?

3. The suffering and glory of Christ are intertwined on the cross. When have you experienced something in your own life that seemed like defeat but later revealed itself as triumph? How might this connect to the paradox of the cross?

4. John's Gospel tells us that Jesus 'gave up his spirit' on the cross—a phrase that can also mean he 'breathed out his Spirit'. How have you experienced the Holy Spirit empowering you to extend Christ's compassion to others?

5. The chapter mentions three contemporary situations (conflict in the Holy Land, climate change, and social injustice) where the cross in our hearts calls us to compassionate action. Which of these or other situations most strongly calls for your response? What specific action might the cross in your heart be prompting?

Spiritual Practices for Holy Week

1. Cross Meditation: Find or create a small cross that you can hold in your hands. Set aside time each day during Holy Week to hold this cross against your heart. As you do, pray slowly: 'Lord Jesus Christ, place your cross deep in my heart, that it may shine in my darkest night'. Remain in silence, aware of Christ's presence within you.

2. Holy Saturday Vigil: On the day between Good Friday and Easter, create a simple vigil practice. Light a candle and place it before a cross. Read John 19:38-42 (the burial of Jesus). Then sit in silence, keeping watch with Christ in the tomb. Allow yourself to experience the waiting, the darkness, the uncertainty that precedes resurrection.

3. Compassionate Action: Choose one specific act of compassion to perform during Holy Week that addresses suffering in your community or world. This might be writing to an elected official about an issue of justice, donating to an organisation serving the vulnerable, or directly serving someone in need. Do this as an expression of the cross you carry in your heart.

Closing Prayer

God of the open heart, revealed to us in Jesus Christ crucified, we come before you with our own hearts laid bare.

We thank you that in what appears to be defeat and humiliation, you have shown us your power and wisdom. In the cross—that instrument of torture and shame—you have revealed the depths of your love and the healing of your grace.

Lord, hear us: *Lord, graciously hear us.*

Place your cross deep within our hearts, not as a burden to bear but as a light to guide us, sparkling like stars in our darkest night. Make our hearts a sanctuary for your presence, breaking open our sealed and guarded places that we might receive you fully.

Lord, hear us: *Lord, graciously hear us.*

As you gave yourself completely for us, help us to give ourselves to you. As your heart was opened for the life of the world, may our hearts be channels of your compassion. Where there is conflict, empower us to work for peace; where there is environmental destruction, empower us to seek renewal; where there is injustice, empower us to seek righteousness.

Lord, hear us: *Lord, graciously hear us.*

May we never forget the cost of our salvation or take for granted the love that bled for us. And may we live as people whose hearts have been forever marked by your cross—people of reconciliation, healing, and hope in a world still yearning for resurrection.

Lord, hear us: *Lord, graciously hear us.*

We pray in the name of Jesus Christ, who died for us and now lives and reigns with you and the Holy Spirit, one God, now and forever. *Amen.*

Afterword

As we come to the end of our journey together through this book, we stand at another threshold. Whether you've read these reflections during Lent, culminating in your meditation on God's open heart on Good Friday, or whether you've explored them during another season of your spiritual life, you may now ask yourself: What next?

Heart work, by its very nature, is never truly finished. Unlike hard work, which can be measured, completed, and set aside, the transformation of our hearts is an ongoing process—sometimes advancing rapidly, sometimes seeming to pause or even retreat, but always continuing as long as we remain open to God's grace.

Since you have begun this work of heart transformation, I invite you to reflect on what God is calling you to do next. The best way to do this is to open our hearts to God and listen to his voice in prayer. God calls each one of us to follow his Son in faithful discipleship. As we have seen in this book, our discipleship is never abstract or theoretical but expressed in both word and deed. The heart that has been opened to receive Christ, naturally would want to seek ways to make him known to others, and partner with him in the work of transforming the world so that it is more closely conformed to God's will.

This calling can take different forms for different people. Some are called to ordained ministry, others to various forms of lay leadership within the church. Many more are called to live out their discipleship in workplaces, families, and communities where Christ's presence is much needed. Whatever your particular calling, it flows from the same source: the heart work that allows God's love to transform you from within.

Hearts that have been broken open to Christ may become increasingly sensitive to the promptings of the Holy Spirit. You may find yourself drawn to new forms of service, challenged to speak out against injustice, or inspired to deepen your prayer life in ways you hadn't previously considered. You might discover gifts you didn't know you had—such as the gift of tears as you mourn the wrongs around you. You might rediscover gifts that have lain dormant—such as my ability to read Dame Julian in her original Middle English which had lain forgotten for thirty years. This is the Holy Spirit at work, as God continuously calls you deeper into discipleship.

I encourage you to remain attentive to these promptings—or 'shewings' as Dame Julian of Norwich calls them. They often begin as a gentle nudge, a persistent thought, or even a holy discontent or righteous anger at the status quo. They may present as discomfort—when I get irritated it is a sign for me to dig deeper to articulate what is moving my heart. They come through Scripture, through the counsel of trusted friends, or through the still, small voice that speaks to us in moments of silence and solitude. Sometimes these promptings arrive as a sudden clarity about a particular need or opportunity—a clear vision. At other times, they emerge gradually as a growing conviction.

Whatever form these promptings take, they invite a response. Heart work invites us to say 'yes' to God's call, even—perhaps especially—when they lead us beyond our comfort zones. Each 'yes' deepens the transformation, creating more space in our hearts for Christ to dwell and work.

As you discern your next steps, please remember that as a member of Christ's body you never have to walk this path alone. The same community that supports us in times of vulnerability and need—just as I experienced after my accident—also travels with us as we respond to God's call. Seek out faith communities that welcome you, where you may find companions who will pray with you, challenge you when necessary, and encourage you when the way seems difficult. And as someone who relies on the gifts and support of others, be open to offer that kind of companion to others on their journeys as well.

Remember also that heart work, while it is deeply personal, always has implications for the community in which you find yourself. As your own heart is transformed, you may become an agent of transformation in your relationships, your community, and potentially in the wider world. The heart that has experienced God's grace naturally seeks to extend that grace to others.

As I review the proofs of this book sixteen weeks after my accident, my physiotherapist has led me through my last session as an outpatient and discharged me formally from our local hospital. My arm is not yet fully recovered; there is still plenty of work to be done, and I leave the physio-department at my hospital with a long list of exercises and strict instructions to continue my twice-weekly remedial personal training and weekly osteotherapy for at least the next three months. The scars of my accident have mostly healed, though one remains as a visible reminder of the beginning of this journey.

Heart work also is never really fully done. In God's eyes all history is present as one, St Augustine knew. The same is true for heart work. We might find ourselves at various stages of heart work at once, or feel that we have to return right back to the beginning, needing to open our hearts anew again and again to God's grace. That, too, is part of the spiritual journey; you may find that you might benefit from re-reading certain chapters of this book again, as you return to your heart work, even long after you have completed and laid aside this book.

My prayer for you is that the heart work begun in these pages will continue to unfold in your life, leading you into ever deeper communion with Christ and ever more faithful service in his name. May you know the joy of a heart that has found its true home in God, and may that joy overflow in love for others.

Our journey of discipleship continues. Our heart work goes on. And the God who has begun this good work in you will surely bring it to completion: 'The God who calls is faithful; and he will accomplish it' (1 Thessalonians 5:24).

A Brief Guide for Book Groups

Getting Started

Before your first meeting, encourage Book Group participants to read the foreword, introduction and first chapter of the book. Consider how you'll structure your time together—will you focus primarily on the reflection questions, or will you incorporate the spiritual practices during your meetings?

Group Discussion Questions on the Book as a Whole

1. **Personal Journey**: Throughout the book, I share how my experience of physical injury and rehabilitation became a metaphor for spiritual heart work. What personal experiences have functioned as metaphors or parables in your own spiritual journey? How have times of vulnerability opened you to deeper transformation?

2. **Contrasting Approaches**: The book contrasts 'hard work' (external achievement) with 'heart work' (internal transformation). In which areas of your spiritual life have you tended towards hard work? Where have you experienced the grace of heart work? How has this book challenged or confirmed your understanding of spiritual growth?

3. **The Heart's Progression**: The book traces a journey from rending our hearts (Ch. 1) through receiving God's word (Ch. 2), asking with courage (Ch. 3), trusting in transformation (Ch. 4), becoming Christ's aroma (Ch. 5), witnessing to others (Ch. 6), and finally receiving the cross into our hearts (Ch. 7). Which of these aspects of heart work resonated most strongly with you? Which challenged you most deeply?

4. From Individual to Community: Heart work begins as an inward, personal journey but inevitably flows outwards into community and witness. How has your group experienced this movement from personal transformation to communal expression? What are some ways your community might embody the heart work you've explored together?

5. Beyond Lent: Though structured as a Lenten devotional, this book invites ongoing heart work beyond the season. What practices or insights from the book do you want to continue exploring? How might you support one another in this continued journey?

Notes and Further Reading

DEDICATION

The scholar remembered by this publication, Benedicta Ward SLG (in secular life Florence Margaret Ward), was born on 4 February 1933 in County Durham and died from cancer on 23 May 2022. A member of a Church of England religious order, the Sisters of the Love of God, since the age of 23, she was a much-loved theologian and historian of the Christian spiritual tradition. Having completed her undergraduate studies at Manchester University, in 1972 she proceeded to study for a doctorate on *Miracles and miracle collections, 1015-1215*, supervised by Sir Henry Southern at the University of Oxford, where her research was based for the rest of her life.

Sister Benedicta's gift as a teacher and theologian was recognised by her Community at Fairacres, who enabled her to be based mostly outside the enclosure of the convent in order to work as reader (a professor without an endowed chair) in early Christian spirituality at the Faculty of Theology and, since 1991, as a Fellow of Harris Manchester College, University of Oxford. A generous teacher, and loyal correspondent with her many past students, she formed and taught generations of undergraduate and graduate students in theology and ecclesiastical history, including the author, whose BA and MPhil, and journey towards the Anglican priesthood, she helped shape.

A most prolific thinker and writer, Sister Benedicta published extensively on the Christian Spiritual tradition, including the following selection of books:

The prayers and meditations of St Anselm (Harmondsworth: Penguin, 1973)

The sayings of the Desert Fathers: the alphabetical collection (London: Mowbray, 1975).

The wisdom of the Desert Fathers: the Apophthegmata Patrum (the anonymous series), Fairacres publications (Oxford: SLG Press, 1975)

The Influence of Saint Bernard: Anglican essays (Oxford: SLG Press, 1976)

Anselm of Canterbury, a monastic scholar: an expanded version of a paper given to the Anselm Society, St. Augustine's College, Canterbury, in May 1973, Fairacres publications (Oxford: SLG Press, 1978)

Liturgy today: the Divine office and the Eucharist, Fairacres publications (Oxford: SLG Press, 1978)

with Kenneth Leech, *Julian Reconsidered*, Fairacres publications (Oxford: SLG Press, 1978)

Miracles and the medieval mind: theory, record and event, 1000–1215 (Aldershot, Hampshire: Scolar Press, 1987)

Harlots of the desert: a study of repentance in early monastic sources (London: Mowbray: 1987)

The desert of the heart: Daily readings with the Desert Fathers (London: Darton, Longman and Todd, 1987)

The Venerable Bede, Outstanding Christian thinkers (London: Chapman, 1990)

Bede and the Psalter (Jarrow on Tyne: Bealls, 1991)

Signs and wonders: saints, miracles, and prayer from the 4th century to the 14th. Collected studies (Aldershot, Hampshire: Variorum, 1992)

High king of heaven: aspects of early English spirituality (London: Mowbray, 1999)

An introduction to Christian spirituality, Ralph Waller, Benedicta Ward eds. (London: SPCK, 1999)

Pilgrimage of the heart, Fairacres publications (Oxford: SLG Press, 2001)

The English mystics revisited (Oxford: Farmington Institute for Christian Studies, 2002)

Joy of heaven: springs of Christian spirituality, Benedicta Ward, Ralph Waller, ed., (London: SPCK. 2003)

Bede, teacher of the English (Oxford: Farmington Institute for Christian Studies, 2004)

A True Easter: The Synod of Whitby 664 AD, Fairacres publications (Oxford: SLG Press, 2007)

Christ within me: prayers and meditations from the Anglo-Saxon tradition (Kalamazoo: Cistercian Publications, 2008)

Anselm of Canterbury: his life and legacy (London: SPCK, 2009)

The Our Father, Fairacres publications (Oxford: SLG Press, 2012)

with Rowan Williams, *Bede's ecclesiastical history of the English people: an introduction and selection* (London: Bloomsbury, 2012)

with Paul Savage and Rozanne E. Elder, *The great beginning of Cîteaux: a narrative of the beginning of the Cistercian order: the Exordium magnum of Conrad of Eberbach*, Cistercian fathers series (Trappist: Cistercian Publications, 2012)

Monastic hours of prayer, Fairacres publications (Oxford: SLG Press, 2016)

In Company with Christ, Fairacres publications (Oxford: SLG Press, 2016)

Give love and receive the Kingdom (Brewster, MA: Paraclete Press, 2016)

ACKNOWLEDGEMENTS

Books and Book Chapters

Andreas Loewe and Katherine Firth, *Journeying with Bonhoeffer: Six Steps on the Path of Discipleship* (Melbourne: Acorn Press, 2024)

Andreas Loewe, *Johann Sebastian Bach's St John Passion (BWV 245): A Theological Commentary—With a New Study Translation by Katherine Firth and a Preface by N.T. Wright* (Leiden: Royal Brill, 2014)

Andreas Loewe and Katherine Firth, 'John in Bach: receiving and telling the gospel of love in and from the heart', in: Chris Skinner and Douglas Estes, eds., *The Reception of John's Gospel* (Waco: Baylor University Press, 2027–29).

CHAPTER 1—THE INWARD JOURNEY OF LENT

Scripture

For further exploration of the heart in Biblical tradition, see Deuteronomy 6:4-6 (the command to love God with all your heart); 1 Samuel 16:7 God looks at the heart rather than outward appearance); Proverbs 4:23 (guarding our hearts); Jeremiah 24:7 (hearts that know God); Ezekiel 36:26 (hearts of flesh for hearts of stone); Matthew 5:8 (the pure in heart); Luke 6:45 (out of the overflow of the heart, the mouth speaks).

Books

St Augustine, *Confessions*, translated by Henry Chadwick (Oxford: Oxford University Press, 2008) is a classic reflection on the restless heart finding rest in God

St Benedict of Nursia, tr. Dom Patrick Barry OSB, *St Benedict's Rule: A New Translation for today* (Ampleforth: Ampleforth Abbey Press, 1997) the basis for many rules of life or rules of monastic communities

David G. Benner, *The Gift of being Yourself: The Sacred Call to Self-Discovery* (Drummers Grove: InterVarsity, 2015) explores how self-knowledge and God-knowledge are intertwined in spiritual transformation

Walter Brueggemann, *Praying the Psalms* (Winona: St Mary's Press, 1993) gives insights into the Psalms as expressions of 'heart work'

St Julian of Norwich, tr. Barry Windeatt, *Revelations of Divine Love* (Oxford: University Press, 2015), the reflections of the fourteenth-century anchorite on the all-pervasive love of Christ

Barbara Brown Taylor, *An Altar in the World: Finding the Sacred beneath our Feet* (Norwich: Canterbury Press, 2009) offers reflections on embodied spirituality

Martin Laird OSA, *Into the Silent Land: A Guide to the Christian Practice of Contemplation* (Oxford: Oxford University Press, 2006) provides a good introduction to the Christian contemplative tradition

Henri Nouwen, *The Return of the Prodigal Son: A Story of Homecoming* (New York: Random House, 1994) explores the spiritual journey of returning to God

Stephanie Paulsell, *Honoring the Body: Meditations on a Christian Practice* (Minneapolis: Fortress Press, 2019) offers practical ways to integrate physical and spiritual awareness

CHAPTER 2—FROM LAW TO FAITH

Scripture

For further exploration of faith and law, see Galatians 2:15-21 (justification by faith, not law); 3:10-14 (Christ redeems from the curse of the law); Ephesians 2:8-10 (saved by grace through faith, not works); Hebrews 4:1-13 (faith leads to God's eternal rest).

Books

St Athanasius, *On the Incarnation, with an Introduction by C.S. Lewis* (Yonkers: St Vladimir's Seminary Press, 1993), a classic defence of Christian doctrine

Dietrich Bonhoeffer, *Discipleship, translated by Barbara Green and Reinhard Krauss* (Minneapolis: Fortress Press, 2015) offers a classic reflection on 'cheap grace' as opposed to 'costly grace'

Sarah Coakley, *God, Sexuality and the Self: An Essay on the Trinity* (Cambridge: Cambridge University Press, 2013) presents systematic theological perspectives on *kenosis* (self-emptying)

Andreas Loewe and Katherine Firth, *Journeying with Bonhoeffer: Six Steps on the Path of Discipleship* (Melbourne: Acorn Press, 2024) provides accessible reflections on Bonhoeffer's teaching on grace

Thomas Merton OCSO, *New Seeds of Contemplation* (Abbey of Gethsemani Inc., 1961) gives insights on moving beyond 'legalism' to a more authentic spiritual life

Richard Rohr OFM, *Falling Upward: A Spirituality for the Two Halves of Life* (London: SPCK, 2013) explores spiritual growth that moves beyond rule-based religion

Fleming Rutledge, *The Crucifixion: Understanding the Death of Jesus Christ* (Grand Rapids: William B. Eerdmans, 2015) reflects on how Christ's work on the cross fulfils the demands of the law

Miroslav Volf, *Free of Charge: Giving and Forgiving in a Culture Stripped of Grace* (Grand Rapids: Zondervan, 2009) offers contemporary reflections on grace

N.T. Wright, *Justification: God's Plan and Paul's Vision* (Drummers Grove: InterVarsity Press, 2016) explores Paul's understanding of faith and justification

CHAPTER 3—THE COURAGE TO ASK

Scripture

For further exploration of prayer, see 1 Samuel 1:9-20 (Hannah's prayer); Luke 11:1-13 (Jesus' teaching on prayer); Luke 18:1-8 (the persistent widow); Philippians 4:6-7 (prayer and anxiety); James 5:13-18 (the prayer of faith).

Books

Walter Brueggemann, *Praying the Psalms* (Winona: St Mary's Press, 1993) gives insights into the full range of human emotion in prayer

John Calvin, *Institutes of the Christian Religion, 1536 Edition*, tr. Ford Lewis Battles (Grand Rapids: Eerdmans, 1995), particularly Chapter III: 'Prayer: With an Exposition of the Lord's Prayer' is relevant here

Richard Foster, *Prayer: Finding the Heart's True Home* (London: Hodder & Stoughton, 1992) explores various forms of prayer across the Christian tradition

Andreas Loewe and Katherine Firth, *Journeying with Bonhoeffer: Six Steps on the Path of Discipleship* (Melbourne: Acorn Press, 2024) gives insights into the poems and prayers of Dietrich Bonhoeffer

Anne P. Lamott, *Help, Thanks, Wow: The Three Essential Prayers* (London: Hodder & Stoughton, 2013) is an accessible reflection on the simplicity and power of Christian prayer

Simone Weil, *Gravity and Grace*, tr. Arthur Wills (Lincoln: University of Nebraska Press, 1952) reflections on being present

Benedicta Ward SLG, *The Desert Fathers: Sayings of the Early Christian Monks* (London: Penguin, 2003) provides a comprehensive introduction to the writings of the founders of monasticism

Samuel Wells, *Incarnational Ministry: Being with the Church* (Grand Rapids: Eerdmans, 2017) on prayer and presence

Philip Yancey, *Prayer: Does It Make Any Difference?* (London: Hodder & Stoughton, 2006) is a thoughtful exploration of the purposes and challenges of prayer

CHAPTER 4—TRANSFORMATION THROUGH TRUST

Scripture

For further exploration of trust in Scripture, see Psalm 27 (God is light and salvation in trouble); Psalm 37:3-7 (committing our ways to God); Proverbs 3:5-6 (trust in God, rather than our own understanding); Isaiah 26:3-4 (perfect peace for those who trust); Jeremiah 17:7-8 (trust leads to blessing and growth); Matthew 6:25-34 (your heavenly Father cares for you); Romans 4:18-22 (Abraham's faith as a model of trust); 2 Corinthians 4:16-18 (unseen eternal realities); Hebrews 11 (the great 'faith chapter').

Books

Author of the Cloud of Unknowing, ed. William Johnstone, *The Cloud of Unknowing and the Book of Privy Counselling* (New York: Crown Publishing, 1973), a classic work on the spiritual loss of self by consciousness on the divine alone

Walter Brueggemann, *The Spirituality of the Psalms* (Minneapolis: Fortress, 2001) explores psalms of trust and orientation

Corrie ten Boom, *The Hiding Place* (Grand Rapids: Baker Publishing, 2023) is a moving autobiography, and memoir of trust, composed during the Holocaust

Jean-Pierre de Caussade, *Abandonment to Divine Providence* (New York: Cosimo, 2007) is a classic seventeenth-century theological reflection on trusting God's will

C.S. Lewis, *A Grief Observed* (New York: Warbler Classics, 2023) is the *Narnia* author's honest wrestling with trust in the midst of suffering following the death of his wife, Joy Davidman

Martin Luther, *Lectures on Romans*, ed. Hilton Oswald, Luther's Works 25 (St Louis: Concordia Press, 1972), the Preface is particularly relevant here

Henri Nouwen, *The Return of the Prodigal Son: A Story of Homecoming* (New York: Random House) explores trust through the lens of coming home to God

CHAPTER 5—THE AROMA OF CHRIST

Scripture

For further exploration of sensory dimensions of faith, see Exodus 30:34-38 (sacred incense); Psalm 45:7-8 (fragrance of God's presence); Song of Songs 1:3 (love as perfume); Ephesians 5:1-2 (fragrant offering); Revelation 5:8 (incense as prayers).

Books

Hans Urs von Balthasar, *The Glory of the Lord: A theological Aesthetics* (San Francisco: Ignatius Press, 1989) includes reflections on the sensory dimensions of faith

St Hildegard of Bingen OSB, *Scivias*, tr. Columba Hart (Mahwah: Paulist Press, 1990) medieval reflections on the senses

John Calvin, *Commentaries on the Epistles of Paul the Apostle to the Corinthians*, tr. John Pringle (Grand Rapids: Baker, 1979) gives insights into the aroma of Christ from the Reformed tradition

Richard Foster, *Prayer: Finding the Heart's True Home* (London: Hodder & Stoughton, 1992) includes reflections on prayer that engages all the senses

Patrick Süskind, *Perfume: The Story of a Murderer* (London: Penguin, 2015), though not a Christian work, powerfully explores the meaning and power of scent

Alexander Schmemann, *For the Life of the World: Sacraments and Orthodoxy* (Yonkers: St Vladimir's Seminary Press, 2018) explores the sacramental nature of all reality

Lauren Winner, *Wearing God: Clothing, Laughter, Fire, and Other Overlooked Ways of Meeting God* (New York: Harper Collins, 2016) offers reflections on God as clothing, bread, and fragrance

CHAPTER 6—THE WITNESSING HEART

Scripture

For further exploration of Christian witness, see Isaiah 43:10-12 (God's people to be his witnesses); Acts 1:8 (witnesses to the end of the earth); 1 Peter 3:15-16 (the hope inside us); Revelation 12:11 (the word of testimony); Matthew 5:13-16 (salt and light); 1 John 1:1-4 (what was seen, heard, and touched).

Books

James H. Cone, *The Cross and the Lynching Tree* (New York: Orbis Books, 2011) reflections on witness to Christ's suffering in Black experience

Shane Claiborne, *The Irresistible Revolution: Living as an Ordinary Radical* (Grand Rapids: Zondervan, 2008) reflections on embodied witness through radical community

Dorothy Day OblSB, *The Long Loneliness* (New York, Harper Collins, 2009) is a powerful memoir of witness through the Catholic Worker movement

Willie James Jennings, *The Christian Imagination: Theology and the Origins of Race* (Yale: Yale University Press, 2010) reflections on witness in a context of racial injustice

Lesslie Newbigin, *The Gospel in a Pluralist Society* (Grand Rapids: William B. Eerdmans, 1988) explores what it means to bear witness in a multifaith context

Desmond Tutu, *No Future Without Forgiveness* (London: Ebury Press, 1999) witness to reconciliation in post-apartheid South Africa

Samuel Wells and Marcia A. Owen, *Living Without Enemies: Being Present in the Midst of Violence* (Drummers Grove: InterVarsity Press, 2011) explores Christian witness in contexts of violence

CHAPTER 7—THE OPEN HEART OF GOD

Scripture

For further exploration of the cross and the heart of God, see Isaiah 53 (suffering servant); Psalm 22 (my God why have you forsaken me); Zechariah 12:10 (the one who has been pierced); John 3:14-16 (God's love shown in his Son); Philippians 2:5-11 (Christ's self-emptying); Hebrews 4:14-16 (Jesus our high priest); Revelation 5:6-14 (the worship of the Lamb that was slain).

Books

Hans Urs von Balthasar, *Mysterium Paschale: The Mystery of Easter* (San Francisco: Ignatius Press, 2012), Christ's abandonment on the cross discloses a 'distance' within God that embraces all human alienation

St Getrude the Great (of Helfta), *The Herald of Divine Love*, tr. Margaret Winkworth (Mahwah: Paulist Press, 1993), perspectives into the medieval devotion to the Sacred Heart

Gustavo Gutiérrez, *A Theology of Liberation* (Maryknoll: Orbis, 1998) God's heart on the cross is wide open for the poor and suffering

Andreas Loewe, *Johann Sebastian Bach's St John Passion (BWV 245): A Theological Commentary—With a New Study Translation by Katherine Firth and a Preface by N.T. Wright* (Leiden: Royal Brill, 2014) gives a detailed account of how Bach came to use Herberger's chorale I quote in this chapter

Alan E. Lewis, *Between Cross and Resurrection: A Theology of Holy Saturday* (Grand Rapids: William B. Eerdmans, 2001) provides a meditation on Holy Saturday and waiting

Jürgen Moltmann, *The Crucified God: The Cross of Christ as the Foundation and Criticism of Christian Theology* (Minneapolis: Fortress, 1993) is a theological classic on how God's identity is revealed in the cross

Fleming Rutledge, *The Crucifixion: Understanding the Death of Jesus Christ* (Grand Rapids: William B. Eerdmans, 2015) offers a theological exploration of the cross

N.T. Wright, *The Day the Revolution Began: Rethinking The Meaning Of Jesus' Crucifixion* (London: SPCK, 2016) on the meaning of the cross

Index

INDEX OF SCRIPTURAL PASSAGES

Old Testament

Genesis

- 15:1-6 (Abraham's trust in God's promise) - 43-46

Deuteronomy

- 30:11-14 (God's word is near) - 15, 17

1 Samuel

- 16:7 (God looks at the heart) - 9

Esther

- Additions to Esther 14:3-14 (Esther's prayer) - 29-31

Psalms

- 22 (My God, why have you forsaken me) - 97
- 27 (God as light and salvation) - 51
- 37:3-7 (Committing our ways to God) - 51
- 45:7-8 (Fragrance of God's presence) - 67
- 51:10 (Create in me a clean heart) - 5, 10

Proverbs

- 3:5-6 (Trust in God, not your own understanding) - 51
- 4:23 (Guarding your hearts) - 9

Isaiah

- 6:5, 8 (Isaiah's commission and call) - 19
- 26:3-4 (Perfect peace for those who trust) - 51
- 43:10-12 (God's people as witnesses) - 81
- 53 (The suffering servant) - 97

Jeremiah

- 17:7-8 (Trust leads to blessing) - 51
- 24:7 (Hearts that know God) - 9

Ezekiel

- 36:26 (Heart of stone to heart of flesh) - 9, 91

Habakkuk

- 2:6, 9-14 (Stones crying out) - 73, 76

Joel

- 2:12-17 (Rend your hearts, not your clothing) - 3-5, 19

New Testament

Matthew

- 5:8 (The pure in heart) - 9
- 5:13-16 (Salt and light) - 81
- 6:25-34 (God's care) - 51
- 7:7-12 (Ask, seek, knock) - 29, 32-33, 35-36

Luke

- 5:8 (Peter's confession of unworthiness) - 20
- 6:45 (From the overflow of the heart) - 9
- 9:20 (Peter's confession of Christ) - 20
- 10:38-42 (Mary and Martha) - 59
- 13:34-35 (Jesus' lament over Jerusalem) - 43, 47-48
- 18:1-8 (The persistent widow) - 37
- 19:29-40 (Triumphal entry into Jerusalem) - 73-75

John

- 1:11 (Jesus comes to his own) - 91
- 3:14-16 (God's love shown in his Son) - 97
- 12:1-8 (Mary anoints Jesus) - 57-60
- 12:28, 32-33, 36, 46 (Jesus lifted up) - 91-92
- 19:16-30 (The crucifixion) - 87-88, 93-94
- 20:27 (Jesus shows his wounds) - 93

Acts

- 1:8 (Witnesses to the ends of the earth) - 81

Romans

- 4:18-22 (Abraham's faith) - 51
- 8:22 (Creation groaning) - 95
- 10:4-13 (Christ is the end of the law) - 15-20

1 Corinthians

- 1:18-25 (The message of the cross) - 87-88, 92
- 4:7 (Treasure in clay jars) - 62

2 Corinthians

- 2:14-17 (The aroma of Christ) - 57, 60-61
- 4:16-18 (Unseen eternal realities) - 51
- 6:1-10 (Now is the day of salvation) - 3, 7

Galatians

- 2:15-21 (Justification by faith) - 22
- 2:19-20 (Crucified with Christ) - 93
- 3:10-14 (Christ redeems from the curse of the law) - 22

Ephesians

- 2:8-10 (Saved by grace through faith) - 22
- 3:17 (Christ dwelling in hearts) - 91
- 5:1-2 (Fragrant offering) - 67

Philippians

- 2:5-7 (Christ's self-emptying) - 47
- 3:17-4:1 (Heavenly citizenship) - 43, 46-47, 49

- 4:6-7 (Prayer and anxiety) - 37

Hebrews

- 4:1-13 (Faith leads to rest) - 22
- 4:14-16 (Jesus our high priest) - 97
- 11 (The 'faith chapter') - 51

James

- 5:13-18 (The prayer of faith) - 37

1 Peter

- 3:15-16 (The hope inside us) - 81

1 John

- 1:1-4 (What was seen, heard, and touched) - 81

Revelation

- 5:6-14 (The worship of the Lamb) - 97
- 5:8 (Incense as prayers) - 67
- 12:11 (The word of testimony) - 81

INDEX OF SUBJECTS AND PEOPLE

Abraham

- faith reckoned as righteousness - 45-46
- looking to the stars - 44-45
- response of trust - 45-46
- sacrifice - 44-46

Aroma of Christ

- as a fragrance that fills the house - 57-60
- different reactions to - 61-62
- living as - 64-65
- qualities of - 59-60

Asking

- courage to - 29-36
- Jesus' teaching on - 32-33
- persistence in - 32-33

Augustine of Hippo - 9, 96, 103

Ávila, Teresa of - 37

Bach, Johann Sebastian

- *St John Passion* - 89-90

Bonhoeffer, Dietrich

- 'costly discipleship' - 81
- *Morning Prayer* - 33-35
- poems and prayers - 33-35
- witness against Nazism - 34, 51

Citizenship in heaven - 46-47

Community

- communal prayer - 34-35
- shared witness - 77-79
- support in vulnerability - 35-36, 49, 102-103

Compassion

- sharing in Christ's suffering - 92-94
- through the cross - 94-95

Courage

- Esther's prayer for - 31
- in asking - 29-36
- of vulnerability - 32-33
- to bear witness - 79

Cross

- as foolishness to the world - 88, 92
- as triumph - 91-92
- in believers' hearts - 90-91
- open heart of God revealed in - 88-89, 95
- placing in our hearts - 89-91

- wisdom and power of God - 88, 92

Desert Fathers and Mothers - 37, 50

Devotion

- extravagant (Mary of Bethany) - 58-60
- fragrance of - 58-60
- vulnerable - 59, 62-63

Discipleship

- costly - 81
- following Jesus to Jerusalem - 47-48
- imitation of Christ - 46-47
- self-emptying - 46-47

Esther (Queen)

- courage to ask - 30-31
- prayer for her people - 30-31
- vulnerability - 30-31

Faith

- and grace - 21-23
- faith in heart and mouth - 19-20
- from law to - 15-22
- through trust - 45-46, 50-51
- transformation through - 49

Fragrance

- aroma of Christ - 57-64
- fragrance of devotion - 58-60
- Mary's perfume - 57-60
- sensory dimension of faith - 66-67

Grace

- for all - 20-21
- living out of - 21-22
- not works - 21-22

Golden Rule (Matthew 7:12) - 35-36

Hard work vs. heart work

- calculation vs. devotion - 61-62
- contrasted throughout - 4-7, 16-19
- external achievements vs. internal transformation - 6-7
- law vs. faith - 16-18

Heart

- as centre of being - 9
- as sanctuary for Christ - 90-91
- believing in - 19-20
- broken open - 5-6, 62-63, 80, 90-91
- cleansing - 5-6
- confessing with mouth - 19-20
- God's heart open on the cross - 88-89, 95
- in Christian tradition - 9-10
- of flesh vs. stone - 90-91
- opened to God - 5-6, 17-18

- transformation of - 7-8, 48-49
- witnessing - 74-80

Hippo, Augustine of - 9, 96, 103

Inward journey

- contrasted with outward observance - 5-7
- interior conversion - 5
- of Lent - 3-8
- rending hearts not garments - 5-6

Julian of Norwich

- 'all shall be well' - 50
- on God's heart - 9, 97
- on prayer - 37

Justice

- climate change - 95
- compassionate action - 77-79, 94-95
- refugee welcome - 77-78
- witness against injustice - 76-77, 95

Kingdom of God

- heavenly citizenship - 46-47
- politics of - 77
- values of - 77, 80
- witnessing to - 79-80

Law

- Christ as the end of - 16-17
- fulfilment of - 16-17
- from law to faith - 15-22
- from law to grace - 22-23

Lent

- as wilderness journey - 4
- inward journey of - 3-8
- purpose of - 5
- transformation during - 7-8

Luther, Martin - 23, 50

Mary of Bethany

- anointing Jesus - 58-60
- extravagant devotion - 58-60
- sitting at Jesus' feet - 59

Norwich, Julian of - see Julian of Norwich

Open heart of God

- at the cross - 88-89, 95-96
- compassion flowing from - 93-94
- revealed in Christ - 89, 95-96

Palm Sunday

- Disciples' witness - 73-75
- stones crying out - 75-76

- triumphal entry - 73-75

Paul (Apostle)

- aroma of Christ - 60-61
- citizenship in heaven - 46-47
- Christ as end of the law - 16-17
- message of the cross - 88

Perfume

- as metaphor for devotion - 58-60
- costly nature of - 59
- fragrance filling the house - 58-60

Prayer

- as courage - 37
- as vulnerability - 33-35
- Bonhoeffer's prayer - 33-35
- communal dimension of - 34-35
- courage to ask - 29-36
- Queen Esther's prayer - 30-31
- from personal to communal - 34-35
- in Christian tradition - 37-38

Presence

- God's presence near us - 17-18
- in suffering - 92-94
- of Christ in believers - 91

Reformation Themes

- faith alone - 23
- grace not works - 22-23
- word made accessible - 17-18

Rehabilitation

- as metaphor for spiritual healing - 6, 49, 96
- author's experience of after physical injury - 3-4, 18-19, 49, 80, 96, 103
- lessons from - 18-19, 49, 80

Resurrection

- cross leading to - 63-64
- hope of - 14, 96
- transformation through - 49, 63

St Paul's Cathedral Melbourne

- refugee welcome banner - 77-78
- witness of the building - 77-78

Spiritual Formation

- heart work - 3-11
- inner transformation - 7-8
- rehabilitation metaphor - 6-7, 18-19
- vulnerability as path - 32-33

Stones

- crying out - 75-76

- hearts of stone to flesh - 90-91
- witnessing to Christ - 75-77

Suffering

- and glory intertwined - 91-92
- compassion through - 92-94
- God's presence in - 92-93
- sharing in Christ's - 92-93

Teresa of Ávila - 37

Transformation

- as ongoing process - 96, 101-103
- from inside out - 7-8
- in Christ - 48-49
- inner work of - 7-8
- through trust - 43-52
- trust as - 48-49

Vulnerability

- and trust - 49, 90-91
- as path to healing - 32-33, 90-91
- courage of - 32-33
- in asking - 32-33
- in prayer - 33-35
- Mary of Bethany's vulnerability - 59

Witness/Witnessing

- as overflow of heart - 74-75

- dimensions of - 78-79
- heart work made visible - 76-77
- in action - 77-79
- of buildings and communities - 77-78
- through suffering - 80, 93-94

Word

- access through Christ - 17-18
- near us - 17-18
- on lips and in heart - 17-19

About this Book

In a world that celebrates achievement and visible success, join the Dean of St Paul's Cathedral Melbourne, The Very Dr Andreas Loewe, on a transformative Lenten journey from 'hard work' to 'heart work'—that profound inner renewal that can happen when people open themselves to God's grace.

Reflecting on the author's own experience of physical injury and rehabilitation, this book explores how our spiritual healing mirrors physical rehabilitation: both require vulnerability, patience, and trust in a process we cannot control. In seven weekly reflections drawing on Scripture, theological insight, and his own personal experience, Dean Andreas guides readers to discover how God can transform us from within when we finally acknowledge that we are not 'fine'; when we realise that we cannot heal ourselves, and that we need God's help.

Drawing on the rich Christian spiritual tradition—from St Augustine of Hippo to Julian of Norwich, to Dietrich Bonhoeffer, and Martin Luther King Jr.—*Heart Work* explores how grace may be found in vulnerability; and encourages readers to begin the inward journey towards transformation. Whether read individually, in groups, or as a church community, this book provides a spiritual framework for embracing the 'heart work' of discipleship—the inner journey that leads, inevitably, to the foot of the cross where we witness not our own work, but God's ultimate heart work revealed in Christ's self-offering for all humanity.

www.ingramcontent.com/pod-product-compliance
Lightning Source LLC
Chambersburg PA
CBHW022042200426
43209CB00072B/1923/J